"Eminently popular in style and practical in aim." —*Christian*

"Marked alike by careful language and sober thought." —*Guardian*

". . . conveys many valuable thoughts, and suggests much that will be profitable to the reader." —*The Universalist Quarterly*

"The theme is one of absorbing interest, and is treated throughout with reverence and perspicuity, while practical lessons are drawn with considerable skill." —*Outlook*

"It is in the pulpit that the secret of [Barrett's] career lies. When the sermon is over . . . our impulse just then is to go home, and in quiet think out the questions between God and our soul which he has raised." —Thomas Robinson, *Evangelical Magazine*

"Theologically and ecclesiastically Mr. Barrett is an earnest Nonconformist, with definite and dogmatic views. In some directions he is a long way in advance of current opinion, be he draws the line very clearly and sharply. Few men maintain so high a level of preaching as he . . . a true priest." —*Christian Age*

"Intended for devotional reading, but of a kind somewhat different from that of the last generation, Mr. Barrett's work, although strictly practical, is written in the light of the latest results in scholarship. It holds firmly by the conclusions of the Evangelical school, and deals chiefly with the psychological problems of the narrative. It is intelligent, reverent, and spiritual, marked by much literary beauty, and will be read with interest by both learned and simple. The temptation of our Lord has been expounded a thousand times; but it has its own special lesson to every generation of men, and when, as here, wisely and reverently and spiritually interpreted, it comes with ever fresh pertinence and power. Its teaching lies close to human life, and Mr. Barrett has applied it with fine discernment, broad sympathies, and excellent literary taste." —*British Quarterly Review*

"And the devil, taking him up into an high mountain, shewed unto him all the kingdoms of the world in a moment of time."
Luke 4:5

# THE TEMPTATION OF CHRIST

GEORGE S. BARRETT

HEATHEN EDITION

**HEATHEN EDITIONS**
THEIR BOOKS. OUR WAY.

Published in the good ole United States of America
by Heathen Editions, an imprint of
Heathen Creative
P.O. Box 588
Point Pleasant, WV 25550-0588

Heathen Editions are available at quantity discounts.
For information and more tomfoolery, check us out online:

heatheneditions.com

@heatheneditions
#heathenedition

First published 1883
Heathen Edition published February 17, 2018
Refreshed February 1, 2023

Heathen logo, colophon, design, Heathenry, and footnotes
Copyright © Heathen Creative, LLC 2018

All rights reserved.

Cover Art: The Temptation of Jesus by Gustave Doré
Book and cover design by Sheridan Cleland
Set in 11pt Garamond Premier Pro
Titles in Afton James

ISBN: 978-1-948316-07-1

FIRST HEATHEN EDITION

## TO THE CHURCH AND CONGREGATION

TO WHOM FOR MANY YEARS

IT HAS BEEN HIS HAPPINESS TO MINISTER,

## THIS VOLUME IS DEDICATED

WITH THEIR PASTOR'S AFFECTION AND RESPECT.

# CONTENTS

Heathenry: A Note on the Text . . . . . . ix
Foreword . . . . . . x
Preface . . . . . . xii
I  The Possibility and the Necessity of the Temptation . . . . . . 1
II  The Reality of the Temptation . . . . . . 11
III  The Instrument and the Divine Ordering of the Temptation . . . . . . 23
IV  The Time and Place of the Temptation . . . . . . 35
V  The First Temptation . . . . . . 49
VI  The Second Temptation . . . . . . 61
VII  The Third Temptation . . . . . . 75
VIII  The Life of Temptation . . . . . . 87
IX  The Ministry of Angels . . . . . . 105
X  Christ's Victory: The Pledge and Power of Our Victory Over Temptation and Sin . . . . . . 117

# HEATHENRY: A NOTE ON THE TEXT

WE'LL hop straight to it: We're entirely aware of the irony in labeling this particular title a "Heathen Edition," and if you are somehow offended by the word "heathen" adorning this book within close proximity of the word "Christ," then a common refrain uttered by our late grandfather jumps to mind: "Simmer down. Be still." You see, the "heathen" of Heathen Editions has nothing to do with religion (or the lack thereof) and everything to do with our cats, whom we affectionately refer to as "heathens" since they do not listen — ever! — and do what they want, when they want, where they want, *however* they want. For anyone who has ever known a cat has surely and quickly deduced that each cat plays by its own rules, and that seemed as worthy an ethos for this publishing venture as any.

Concerning the text, we've used the original 1883 MacNiven & Wallace text, but for clarity and readability's sake we've abandoned all of the British spellings (many were archaic) for their modern, American equivalents, except those quoted from the King James Version of the Bible. We've also swapped all Bible verse Roman numerals for their Arabic parallels. And, in addition to our own annotations, we've researched, revised, clarified, and expanded on the original footnotes to include further information as well as additional publication details for the various texts that Barrett references.

Our cats do not care in the least, but we believe our version is certainly a marked improvement upon the original and we sincerely hope you enjoy reading it as much as we have.

# FOREWORD

THE current number of the *Christian Age* contains a photograph of the Rev. George S. Barrett, B.A., and an appreciative biographical sketch. The writer, who remarks that "in Norwich, Nonconformity is very strong, and its influence very great," adds that, "This is mainly owing to the fact that the churches have had a remarkable apostolical succession of blue and Godly pastors. In the Baptist Church of St. Mary's the ministry of Kinghorn, Brock, and Gould extended over more than half-a-century. The beloved and honored predecessor of Mr. Barrett at Prince's Street Church, the Rev. J. Alexander, labored in the same place for fifty years. Mr. Barrett himself has had but one charge." From Mr. Barrett's biography in brief, it appears that he was born in Jamaica in 1839, being the son of a Congregational missionary, and came to England in 1849. At University College, London, he studied mathematics and classics under De Morgan and F. W. Newman, and his thoughts turned to the medical profession, for which he began to qualify himself. But the hand of God was strong upon him, and he felt that his life must be given to the cure of souls. He entered Lancashire Independent College in 1862, and took his B.A. degree at London University. In 1866 he accepted the pastorate of Prince's Street Church, and his ministerial career has been uninterruptedly successful. Having described the manifold activities carried on by the Church, and the erection of the lecture hall and schoolrooms, the sketch concludes with this tribute to Mr. Barrett's power and usefulness: "His contributions to periodical and more permanent literature have been considerable. His chief works are *The Temptation of Christ* in the Household Expositor Series, and a volume of Prayers

FOREWORD    xi

for use in the home. He is now about to issue a volume of sermons. But it is in the sphere of hymnology that he has rendered the greatest service to the churches generally, especially to those of his own communion. He has edited three hymnals, which certainly, from the point of view of the music, taste, breadth of sympathy and harmony with Congregational worship, hold the field against all competitors. In the judgment of the present writer, no other book can compare with the *Congregational Church Hymnal* which Mr. Barrett has issued. But after all it is as a preacher and pastor that one thinks of him. Few men maintain so high a level of preaching as he. There is no padding in his sermons. He aims at producing a certain effect. He is never content unless he has some speculative, practical, or spiritual end before him. He sees the heart of his text and subject and rarely misses his way. Equally helpful is the devotional service, and his prayers flow manifestly from a heart which is filled with God. Amid so many labors it would not be strange if pastoral work were neglected; but it is not so. He is diligent and systematic in visitation. Without a vestige of sacerdotalism he is a true priest — sincerely sympathetic, free alike from harshness and levity, deeply spiritual; the weary, the sick, the bereaved, and the sinful find it easy to tell their tale into his ear, and they never tell it in vain. Theologically and ecclesiastically Mr. Barrett is an earnest Nonconformist, with definite and dogmatic views. In some directions he is a long way in advance of current opinion, be he draws the line very clearly and sharply. He is absolutely loyal to the Evangelical faith broadly interpreted. He is a Congregationalist because he is a Churchman in the true sense of the term. He is intolerant of negations, vulgarities, half-truths, and the dissidence of dissent. He is fitted indeed by his charm of manner, culture, and piety to be a mediating influence among some who do not look with a very sympathetic eye upon dissent. Many attempts have been made to draw him from Norwich, but so far they have failed."

*The Norfolk News*
No. 2469 (p. 5)
April 6, 1892

# PREFACE

THE substance of this volume was delivered in the ordinary course of my ministry to the church and congregation to whom I have ventured to dedicate it. That it retains traces of its original character, I am fully aware; but as this series is entitled "The Household Library of Exposition," and is intended rather for family reading than for the discussion of any of the great critical or theological questions connected with Scripture, I have not cared to remove altogether from the book that practical coloring which is appropriate to most sermons. At the same time I trust that this attempt to expound the Temptation of Christ, in its relation both to Himself, and to our own temptations, will not altogether fail of the character of an "exposition" properly so called. It is impossible to study, for any length of time, any part of the life or words of the Lord Jesus Christ, without being painfully conscious how far short of their infinite meaning all our thoughts and words ever fall; and no one can feel this, in regard to the present volume, more keenly than myself. If, however, this little book brings any of its readers nearer to Him of Whom it chiefly speaks; if it enables them to feel more deeply the reality of His humanity, and the greatness of the sacrifice and of the struggle He undertook in the redemption of the world; if it helps any soul "sore beset of sin" to fight more courageously "the good fight of the faith," and to rely more trustfully on the sympathy and help of Him, Who "in that He Himself suffered being tempted, is able to succor them that are tempted," I shall be thankful that, with whatsoever imperfections, I have been permitted to publish it.

It only remains to say that the quotations from the New Testament are all taken from the 'Revised Version;" a version which, in spite of some defects in rhythm, and occasionally a too minute scrupulosity of scholarship, I regard as the most precious, because the most faithful, translation of the Book of Life yet given to the English speaking nations of the world.

George S. Barrett
Norwich, May 1883

"For it became Him, for whom are all things, and through whom are all things, in bringing many sons unto glory, to make the author of their salvation perfect through sufferings."
Hebrews 2:10

# I
## THE POSSIBILITY AND THE NECESSITY OF THE TEMPTATION

BEFORE entering on any exposition of the Temptation of Christ as recorded for us in the Gospels, there are some preliminary questions of grave importance which demand our serious consideration.

Assuming for the time the account of the temptation given by the evangelists, it may be asked how was temptation possible to Christ, or if its abstract possibility be conceded, how could it in any way have been necessary for Him to have passed through any personal conflict with the Tempter, seeing that from the first hour of His human life to its last, He was "holy, guileless, undefiled, and separated from sinners." We can readily understand the necessity for so sharp a discipline as temptation in our own case, because we are conscious of impurity and imperfection, and these are often so intimately mixed up with our character and life that nothing but the most searching fire — and temptation is such a fire — can separate the dross from the gold; but why should Christ have needed the fire, seeing there was no dross to be separated from the gold in Him? Was not the Lord Jesus — for this is what the question really comes to — too good to be tempted?

It is to the consideration and discussion of this question we now invite attention.

There can be no doubt that if the Lord Jesus Christ had not become incarnate He would never have been tempted, and for the simple reason that temptation is not possible to God. St. James tells us that

## THE TEMPTATION OF CHRIST

"God cannot be tempted with evil,"[1] and although the literal accuracy of the translation, which both the "Authorized," and the "Revised" Versions have given of the original[2] may be open to question, still there is no doubt that the Greek fairly bears the meaning given to it in our version, even though it should mean something more as well. Probably the nearest English equivalent would be "inexperienced in evil," and a Being who has no personal experience of evil must necessarily be an untempted and untemptable Being. In fact we cannot conceive of God being tempted. Temptation involves, as we shall see, the possibility of yielding to it, and therefore of sin, but we can no more think of the possibility of God sinning than we can think of the possibility of God ceasing to exist. Necessary Being and necessary Goodness are equally inseparable from our idea of God, and although it may be difficult for us to understand how a Being Whose nature is necessarily good can possess, as we believe God possesses, a will which is everlastingly free, and which freely chooses that which is good, yet the solution of the difficulty is not to be found in the denial of either of these apparently contradictory truths, but in a higher truth, possibly inconceivable by us, which harmonizes and reconciles them both.

God is above the possibility of temptation.

But if God is above temptation the beasts are below it.[3] It is impossible to think of a beast being tempted, but for the opposite reason to that which made it impossible to think of God being tempted. God is too high, but the beasts are too low, to be tempted.

They are removed from the possibility of falling below their own nature by being placed on so low a level that a fall from it is impossible. God, on the other hand, is equally removed from the possibility of falling, but through the possession of a Nature which by its eternal and necessary goodness places Him too high for even the approach of evil. The "beasts that perish" are at one end of the scale of being, while the Infinite and Eternal God is at the other, and of neither is

---

[1] James 1:13
[2] ἀπείραστος.
[3] I owe this thought to Principal A. M. Fairbairn's suggestive studies of the Temptation published in the *The Catholic Expositor and Literary Magazine*, Vol. III (1876).

temptation thinkable. But with man the case is altogether different. Standing midway between God and the lower animals, allied in one part of his nature with God above, and in another part with the beasts below him, with a lower and a higher nature ever contending for the mastery within him, by the very constitution of his nature man is necessarily a temptable being. He may rise to the Divine Image, or he may sink into the mere animal, but which of these two opposing alternatives shall be his final destiny can be revealed only by trial. And hence temptation is not an accidental incident of man's existence on earth, it is an essential part of that state simply because it is a state of probation. The gracious purposes which temptation is made to fulfill in the spiritual training and perfecting of his nature we shall consider later on; it is sufficient now to emphasize the fact that by the very conditions and laws of our nature we are subject, and necessarily subject to temptation. We are not above it, as God is: nor are we below it, as the beasts are: we are in it, as men.

Nor is this all. The possession of an animal nature is not the only possible source of temptation, or the "angels who kept not their own principality" would never, and could never, have fallen. It would seem that the conditions of any moral goodness possible to a creature necessarily involve the possibility of its opposite. For what is goodness? It is not doing the will of God, or the sun and stars would have a right to claim this glory for themselves: it is the doing the will of God by a will free to obey, and free therefore to disobey, that will. The only conception we can form of spiritual goodness in man is of his voluntary and glad submission to the will of God; if the will be coerced into obedience, goodness is at an end. Goodness, both toward God and toward man, ceases the moment its opposite becomes impossible; and hence the highest and the spiritual part of man's nature, his will, must necessarily be as temptable as his lowest and animal nature. In fact, the most perilous temptations which assault us are not exhausted in the sins of the flesh. Pride, avarice, vain glory, malice, hatred, and all uncharitableness, are distinctly spiritual sins, and for their motives appeal to a region of man's nature far removed from his bodily appetites. In whatever way we regard man, so far as his existence here is concerned, temptation is inseparable from our idea of goodness.

It would seem, therefore, that if the Lord Jesus was "in all points made like unto His brethren, yet without sin," one part of His voluntary assumption of our human nature must have been his submission to temptation. Lifted above temptation as the eternal Son of God, Christ deliberately put Himself within its reach by becoming the Son of Man. To say that Christ was temptable is really only another way of saying that Christ was man. The possibility of His being tempted, and the reality of his humanity, are inseparably conjoined. But even this does not fully meet the difficulty which surrounds the temptation of our Lord — it may explain its possibility; it does not justify its necessity. We need temptation because of the imperfection and sinfulness of our natures; but for this very reason it would seem to have been needless for Christ. Was He not, as has already been asked, too good to be tempted?

Now to this difficulty two sufficient replies may be given.

In the first place, all human goodness needs the strain of temptation *to reveal* its reality and depth. Even when that goodness, as in the case of the Man Christ Jesus, and in His case alone, is absolutely without fault or imperfection, temptation is still required to prove its strength, and by the proof to reveal the depth and solidity of its foundations in the soul. The ship that lies at anchor in the harbor when hardly a breath of wind ripples the surface of the water, may hold to her moorings, but this is no proof of the strength and soundness of her cable, for no strain has been put upon it; but if she is out at sea, and caught in a furious storm, and drifting fast on to a lee shore,[4] and then lets go her anchor, and it holds, there is proof enough of the quality of her cable. The soldier who marches proudly along on a review day may be a brave man at heart, and a good soldier, but no one can be sure of it. See him under fire in actual battle, and you will know in a moment of what stuff he is made. Just so temptation is at once a test and a revelation of all true goodness. No doubt it may

---

[4] A shore toward which the wind blows and toward which a ship is likely to be driven.

reveal, and often does reveal to us, unsuspected weaknesses and flaws in the character, just as the storm at sea may show the rottenness of the cable by snapping it, or the battlefield may prove the soldier to be a coward, but we cannot avoid this. All proof involves risk, the risk of discovering weakness as well as strength, but there is no other way of being assured there is no weakness to be discovered.

Here, then, is the first great reason for the necessity of temptation: man needs it, not because he is fallen and sinful, but because he is man. Had Adam never fallen, every child of Adam would have required the same discipline which their first parents passed through to test the reality of his loyalty to God. The tree of forbidden fruit would have been found in every Paradise.

We may now see how it was that the Lord Jesus Christ in becoming man voluntarily subjected Himself to the discipline of temptation. It tested and revealed, as it alone could, the inner allegiance of His human soul to God. The struggle with the tempter, prolonged for forty days, and culminating at the hour of greatest weakness in the great temptations recorded in the Gospels, was at once the proof that He who came forth victorious from such a conflict was no holiday soldier, no make-believe hero, but in very deed and truth "the Captain of our salvation," Himself foremost in the thickest and fiercest fight; and also the proof that if in such a fight no weak places in His armor were discovered, it could only have been because there were none to be found. The majesty and glory of the human goodness of Jesus were never seen more brightly than when He came forth from the wilderness victorious over every assault which the craft and malignity of Satan could devise, "tempted in all points like as we are, yet without sin."

But temptation accomplishes more than the revelation of the reality of goodness, *it positively strengthens goodness by assaulting it.* To say that a man who has been met by some subtle inducement to evil, and who has refused to yield to it, although at the cost of personal loss and suffering, has shown the reality of his goodness, is only to say half the truth. He has not only maintained his former goodness unimpaired, but he has received new moral strength from the very act of resisting evil. He is a stronger and a better man than he was before he was assaulted by the tempter. We cannot pass through any temptation and come out of it morally unaltered. We may yield to it, in which case we have done more than sin against God, we have made the next act of sin easier by weakening the strength of the will, and by deadening the keenness and sensitiveness of the conscience; or we may resist it and overcome it, but then the victory is more than a victory, it has actually multiplied the forces of righteousness within us, and has made the next victory easier, and the next sin harder, by the moral strength which it has imparted to the whole character. There are some shells which cling to the rocks in spite of the continual buffeting of the tides, but these shells are thickest and strongest where the tide has smitten them with its fullest might, and just so the defenses of the soul against evil grow firmer, and its armor of righteousness becomes more formidable, in proportion to the evil which has been resisted and victoriously overcome.

And this is why no human character becomes stable or strong in goodness until it has been exposed to temptation. Shield it from all the fierce blasts of temptation, preserve it in a forced isolation from the world, and it will remain as unstable as water beneath a summer sky: but let the rough frosts of winter fall on it, and the biting winds lash it, and it will slowly knit itself into compact and solid strength, and like the ice, will defy the storm which has only given it strength by attacking it. Christian parents sometimes fondly wish that it were possible for them to preserve their children through life from all experience of the evil which they know too well awaits them in the great world without, and that they could throw around the conscience of childhood a shield, through which no assaults of temptation could pierce, but they could hardly wish for their children a more unwise or fatal boon. To preserve goodness from being assaulted by evil, is to endanger the stability and growth of goodness itself; for just as plants which have been reared in a hothouse, and shielded from every wintry blast, are never strong, but are in danger of being cut off by the first frost they have to endure, so children who have been brought up in an unnatural and artificial atmosphere of piety, who have been guarded by mistaken parental love from those recurring conflicts with evil which, however slight in themselves, are enough to test a child's strength — and are intended by a merciful Providence to develop that strength by testing it — are often the first to make "shipwreck of faith," and sometimes of moral character itself, when they have to endure the sharp discipline of personal contact with the world, and with the evil that is in the world.

"Blessed," says St. James,[5] — and as we read the words we cannot forget he was our Lord's brother after the flesh, and may have been thinking of this conflict in the wilderness as he wrote them — "is the man that endureth temptation," and we may still repeat the same words.

He is "blessed" if he "endures temptation" — not if he yields to it — because each assault of the tempter has strengthened the faith it was intended to destroy. He is "blessed" because he comes forth from the conflict a nobler and a stronger man. The storm which threatened to tear the tree from the mountainside has only made it drive its roots the deeper down, and has strengthened its anchorage there.

All this is true of the temptation of the Lord Jesus Christ. There are deep words in the Epistle to the Hebrews, the full meaning of which we cannot grasp, which speak of Jesus having been "made perfect through sufferings," of His having "learned obedience by the things which He suffered," and we may understand something of the meaning of these words when we read them in the light of the temptation in the wilderness.

Temptation did for Jesus what it does for all who overcome it by the grace of God. He emerged from the deadly conflict with Satan, lifted, so far as His human goodness was concerned, to a loftier moral greatness, a surer and more commanding strength, than would have been possible without the struggle. Not without the deepest meaning does St. Luke conclude his account of the temptation with these significant words, "And Jesus returned IN THE POWER OF THE SPIRIT into Galilee."[6] But we have not yet exhausted the meaning

[5] James 1:12
[6] Luke 4:14

and purpose of our Lord's temptations. We have seen their value to Himself as a personal discipline through which His human character needed to pass, at once to test and to confirm the reality of its goodness, but this is not the only value they had. They had a representative as well as a personal significance, as being the temptations and the victory of One who was not only "the man Christ Jesus," but the Elder Brother and Head of the whole human race. Christ was "the Son of Man." This name was His own name for Himself; a title never used until He created it, and, with one significant exception,[7] never used in the New Testament except by Christ Himself. It was a title which in one pregnant word expressed not only the true humanity of the Lord Jesus, but His eternal and universal relation to humanity as a whole; the unique character of His own humanity as summing up and therefore representing all that belonged to humanity as such, and as revealing for the first time to the world the beauty and nobleness of that ideal goodness of which human nature was capable, and which was hinted in the great words which accompanied the creation of Adam, "Let us make man in our image, after our likeness;" The life of Jesus, in this aspect, was as truly a representative life, as His death was a representative death: it was the life, in a word, of One who as really represented man to God as He represented God to man.

It is in this light that the temptation and the victory of Christ reach their last and fullest significance. Christ came to restore a fallen race to its loyalty to God; He came to redeem a world of sinners from their sin; to "destroy the works of the devil," and in the place of the usurping kingdom of Satan to set up once more, and on foundations which should never again be shaken, the everlasting kingdom of heaven.

And the first public and official act of Him who was the Redeemer and Savior of the world is to encounter the head and representative of the kingdom of evil, to be assaulted by his most furious malice, but to come forth from the conflict not vanquished but victor. The first victory of the new Head of Humanity over the devil is at once the prophecy and the pledge of His final triumph over sin, and of His

---

[7] The exception is in the dying speech of Stephen, Acts 7:56.

redemption of the race with which He had now forever identified Himself, from "the bondage of corruption" into "the liberty of the glory of the children of God."

But the victory of Christ over the devil becomes even more significant when it is contrasted with the fall of Adam. Adam was the first head and representative of humanity, and as such had to endure, as Christ endured, the temptation of the devil. But in everything else how unmeasurably unlike were "the first" and "the second Adam." Adam fell; Christ conquered, and conquered although He was beset by a fierceness of assault Adam never knew: conquered, although fighting at a disadvantage Adam never experienced.

Adam was tempted in a garden. Christ was tempted in a wilderness. Adam was tempted in the fullness of bodily strength, and when feebleness and infirmity of the flesh gave no edge to the sword of the tempter. Christ was tempted when worn and weakened by a fast that had lasted without interruption for forty days. Adam was tempted once. Christ was "forty days tempted of the devil," the long, persistent assaults of the devil culminating in the three final and typical temptations the details of which are preserved to us in the Gospels. And finally, Adam fell; but Christ overcame.

It is the first great act of the redemption of the race from sin. It is the first clarion note that announces the advent of the new Head of humanity, the Redeemer of the world. It is the first conclusive defeat of the kingdom of darkness in that holy war which shall never end until "the end shall come" and the "kingdom of the world become the kingdom of our God and His Christ," who "shall reign for ever and ever."[8]

The shame and reproach of our first parents' fall are already rolled away, and as the Son of Man returns from this mighty conflict in the wilderness with the prince of darkness, victorious in every assault, we may hear even from these desert sands a voice sounding in every dungeon bidding the prisoners, long held captive by Satan, "Lift up your heads because your redemption draweth nigh."[9]

---

[8] Revelation 11:15
[9] Luke 21:28

"Who in the days of his flesh, having offered up prayers and supplications with strong crying and tears unto him that was able to save him from death, and having been heard for his godly fear, though he was a Son, yet learned obedience by the things which he suffered."

Hebrews 5:7–8

# II

# THE REALITY OF THE TEMPTATION

ADMITTING the possibility and even the necessity of temptation as a moral discipline for the Man Christ Jesus, the still graver question at once arises of its reality. Did our Lord undergo as real a struggle with the tempter during His temptation in the wilderness as that which we have to wage during our earthly life; or, on the other hand, was the temptation merely a dramatic exhibition[1] to the mind of Christ of the seductions and allurements to evil which beset us, so as to give Him a vivid sense of the conflicts through which we have to pass on our pilgrimage, but not so as to involve Him in any personal conflict with, or peril from, the powers of darkness and of evil? On the answer that is given to this momentous question depends the entire moral significance of the temptation, both in its relation to our Lord and in its relation to man, and it demands, therefore, the most careful and reverent consideration.

One thing seems, at the outset, to be tolerably certain. If we take the accounts of the temptation as they are given to us in the three Gospels which relate it, there can be no doubt that the Evangelists were thoroughly convinced of its reality. The whole tone of their narrative, quite as much as the statements which they make about the

---

[1] This is apparently the view taken of the temptation of our Lord by the late Professor Henry Rogers in his remarkable work *The Superhuman Origin of the Bible* (1874). Mr. Rogers says (p. 178) — "Nor is it difficult to show that, however impeccable, He might at least receive from the *presentation* of temptation — under the pressure or those sufferings and privations which so generally give it power over us — that vivid sense of *our* temptations, and of the conflicts they necessitate, which only experience can impart."

temptation, is unmistakable evidence of their conviction that the temptation was as real to Christ as our temptations are to us. So, too, the other references which are found in the New Testament to the temptation all point in the same direction. The author of the Epistle to the Hebrews, for instance, declares that Christ "was in all points tempted like as we are, yet without sin,"[2] an assertion which would be untrue in its most important particular, if Christ had not personally felt the terrible strain of the struggle with evil which confers on our temptations their deepest reality and bitterness. In another place in the same Epistle we are also told that Christ "suffered, being tempted,"[3] and it seems difficult, if not impossible, to imagine that the only meaning the writer intended by such an expression was, that Christ suffered when He realized what our temptations were, and not that He suffered in the fierceness of His own conflict with evil. "The Captain of our salvation" must surely have Himself been foremost in "the good fight of faith." With statements like these before us it is not wonderful that the Church of Christ has always refused to accept any explanation of the temptation which reduced it to an unreality, and myriads of weak and tempted souls' in their hour of peril have drawn strength and courage to resist "all the fiery darts of the evil one," from the remembrance of One who "in that He Himself suffered, being tempted, is able to succor them that are tempted."

There is, moreover, another point of view from which the temptation of our Lord may be regarded, and which serves to confirm our belief in its reality.

Assuming, for the time, the personal existence of that being whom Scripture calls "the devil," "the prince of the power of the air," "the old serpent," "Satan," — and it is difficult, if not impossible, to understand how anyone who acknowledges the authority of the Lord Jesus Christ and of His apostles can have any doubt on this point — is it conceivable for a single moment that such a being would have engaged in conflict with Christ unless he had known the conflict was to be a real and awful one on both sides? Can we imagine the tempter

---

[2] Hebrews 4:15
[3] Hebrews 2:18

*playing at fighting* with Christ as if they were the opposing sides of a friendly army on a great review day? The supposition is impossible; and we shall have occasion hereafter to point out how immeasurably the significance of the temptation of our Lord is increased when we consider it in its relation, too often overlooked or forgotten, to the devil himself, whose supreme aim it was to defeat, at the very outset of our Lord's mission, Him who had expressly come "to destroy the works of the devil." The reality of the tempter demands the reality of the temptation.

But the moment we admit the reality of the temptation to Christ another and a still graver question arises. The reality of our temptations lies in the terrible fact that they are temptations to SIN, and necessarily therefore involve the possibility of our falling before them into sin; so that if we admit Christ's temptations were real, does not this involve the awful possibility of His yielding to them; or in other words, if we may use for a moment the theological term which expresses this possibility, must not a tempted Christ be a peccable[4] Christ?

There can be little doubt that our first impulse is to answer this question instantly in the negative. Our reverence for the glory and dignity of the person of the Lord Jesus, the worship and adoration we pay to Him as the personal manifestation of the unseen and eternal God, the perfect holiness and beauty of His human character, all combine to make the bare suggestion of the possibility of Christ yielding to temptation, and therefore of Christ sinning, so unspeakably repulsive and painful, that we dismiss it at once as bordering on blasphemy.

And yet deeply as every Christian heart must sympathize with the sensitive jealousy for the honor of its Lord shown in such a reply, it is not difficult to show that not only is the majestic moral grandeur of Christ's victory over temptation, with all the great lessons it involves, taken away if we deny the possibility of His yielding to the tempter — so that instead of honoring, we really dishonor Him by the denial — but that both those who affirm it was possible for Christ to sin,

---

[4] Capable of sinning; susceptible to temptation.

and those who say it was impossible, will be found when we carefully examine their meaning really to mean the same thing.

Let us take this latter point first of all. What, then, is meant when it is said it was impossible for Christ to have sinned?

Certainly not that it was a physical impossibility, as when we say it is impossible for a man surrounded with every comfort and luxury to feel the temptation a starving man feels to steal a loaf of bread, for in addition to the physical impossibility of temptation being utterly meaningless in the case of our Lord, and contradicted by the circumstances under which the very first temptation took place, it would have at once destroyed the temptation itself. A temptation the yielding to which is a physical impossibility, is a contradiction in terms.

It follows, therefore, that those who say it was impossible for Christ, as man, to sin, must mean by this that it was a moral impossibility. But granting this, what is a moral impossibility of sinning? What do we mean, for example, when we say of someone whom we may know, and whose whole life has borne witness to his transparent integrity and honor, that it is impossible for him to tell a lie? Do we not mean that we are so certain of our friend's loyalty to truth, of the attitude of his moral nature to everything false or deceitful, that we are sure that no pressure of temptation would ever induce him to depart from the path of rectitude and truth? In like manner, but with an assurance as infinitely greater as the moral character of Christ is infinitely holier than that of the most saintly of His servants, when we say it was impossible for Christ to yield to temptation, we mean we are so sure of His perfect holiness, of His utter abhorrence of all evil, of the absolute harmony of His will with His Father's, as to make it "impossible" for Him to yield, even in thought for one single moment, to the faintest suggestion of evil. He could have yielded if He had chosen, but we know He never would have chosen.

On the other hand, when it is said on the opposite side that it was possible for Christ to have sinned, the word "possible" carries with it an ambiguity of meaning that has an evil sound. It seems to suggest what might, or might not, occur, as for example when we say it is possible for even the best Christian to make mistakes, meaning that we can never be sure a Christian will not sometimes err.

But this secondary and evil implication of the word "possible" has no conceivable application to the Lord Jesus Christ. When we say it was "possible for Him to sin" we never mean that we are not sure whether He will, or will not sin. We do not imply, as in the case of a fellow creature, any uncertainty as to the result. We are certain of the result, whatever temptation comes to Christ, because we are certain of the inflexible adherence of His will to the will of God and of His immovable loyalty to the eternal law of righteousness and truth. For Him an eternal temptation would only have meant an eternal victory. He could have yielded, if He had chosen, but He never would have chosen to yield. It was possible for Him to sin, and yet impossible; possible if He had chosen, impossible for Him to have chosen.

Now if this be a true account of the two sides which have been taken in this controversy as to the peccability of Christ, considered as man, it will be seen that both sides are really one. Those who most strenuously deny the possibility of Christ yielding to temptation are found, on inquiry, to mean that it was the sublime moral impossibility of a will in perfect accord with the will of God even to choose evil; while those who maintain that He could have yielded, had He chosen, are found to be equally resolute in declaring He never would have chosen, because of His immovable fidelity to His Father's will. The question we have been considering is one which has long been discussed by theologians under the form of the antithetical alternative whether Christ was "not able to sin," or was "able not to sin." If the course of reasoning we have been pursuing be correct, the opposing members of this alternative turn out to be only different ways of stating the same thing. He was "not able to sin" simply because He was "able not to sin."

But if the reality of the temptation of Christ be conceded to involve at least the abstract possibility of His having yielded, had He chosen, to the tempter, then some further difficulties arise which deserve thoughtful and serious attention. It may be asked, in the first place, how the temptability of Christ can be reconciled with

His essential Divinity; or in other words, if Christ were none other than the God-Man, how is it possible ever to conceive of Him as approached and assaulted by temptation? Now there is but one reply to this difficulty, that we have here two truths, either of which seems utterly irreconcilable with the other, and both of which nevertheless are true. We cannot conceive of the true Deity of Christ without shutting out all possibility of temptation: we cannot conceive of His true humanity without admitting that possibility: but these apparently incompatible truths are only part of the greater mystery of the Incarnation itself. We cannot conceive how the omnipresence of God localized and limited itself in the person of the man Christ Jesus: nor how the omniscience of God could dwell in One whose human soul "grew in wisdom;" nor how the eternal blessedness of God was possible in One who was "a man of sorrows and acquainted with grief;" nor how God could become man and die on the cross. We are, in fact, face to face here with the final mystery of the Infinite becoming the Finite, and all we can do is to confess the utter inability of the human reason to comprehend so transcendent and awful a descent. But just as we believe in the humanity of our Lord, although it may be impossible to reconcile it with His Divinity; and just as we believe in His Divinity without being able to reconcile it with His humanity, so we hold at once the untemptability of the God, but the temptability of the man Christ Jesus. All the difficulties involved in His liability to temptation finally run up into, and are lost in the vaster mystery of the union of the Divine and the Human in the single and unique personality of the God-Man, Christ Jesus.

But again, it may be asked whether the consciousness of temptation is not in itself an admission of moral imperfection, and if so, whether it is not inconsistent with the perfect holiness of the human character of the Lord Jesus Christ to imagine temptation being a reality to Him.

To this we may reply that everything depends on the origin and source of the temptation. It may arise — it does often arise — in our own case, from our own hearts; a man may be "drawn away," as St.

## THE REALITY OF THE TEMPTATION  17

James says, "by his own lust, and enticed,"[5] and in such a case, no doubt, the fact of temptation arising, and of its assault being felt, is itself an evidence of moral imperfection within. If we were absolutely sinless and pure, if no fatal bias or tendency to evil lurked in the secret places of our will, no temptation could arise from within; there would be no foes "of our own household" to contend against, and any attack on our fidelity and loyalty to God would have to be made from without. The fact that many of our most deadly temptations are generated in the unholy desires and passions of our own evil hearts, and even when not actually arising there, but coming from seeds of evil sown by "an enemy" external to us, spring up when once the seed is sown, like poisonous weeds in a congenial soil, is doubtless one of the saddest proofs of the sinfulness of our human nature, and of the immeasurable distance it has fallen from "the image of God" in which it was originally created.

But temptation may arise, and often does arise, not from within but from without. Evil men may tempt us, or Satan himself may directly tempt us, and in either case the consciousness of temptation is not sin. It is, as we saw in the last chapter, one of the essential conditions of a state of probation that it should be a state of temptation, and temptation therefore no more necessarily involves the idea of sin than probation does. If man had never fallen but had remained steadfast in his obedience to God, so long as probation lasted he would still have required temptation to test and to consolidate the moral value of that obedience, even though all the inducements to sin came to him only from without.

It will be seen, therefore, that the access of temptation to the soul is not necessarily any proof of moral imperfection unless the temptation originally arises from within the soul itself. But all Christ's temptations came to Him not from within, but from without. Each of the Gospels which record the temptation is careful to tell us that when Jesus was tempted He was tempted by the devil. "Then was Jesus led up of the Spirit into the wilderness to be tempted of the devil;" "He

---

[5] James 1:14

was in the wilderness forty days tempted of Satan;" He was "led by the Spirit in the wilderness during forty days, being tempted of the devil," are the significant words which are found at the commencement of the account of the temptation in the Gospels of St. Matthew, St. Mark, and St. Luke respectively.[6] None of Christ's temptations arose from within, there were no traitors in the garrison secretly aiding the foe without; and for Him, therefore, to be assaulted by seduction to evil as little implied any moral imperfection in His own character, or any inward disloyalty to God, as the siege of a beleaguered fort by an invading army implies that the garrison defending it are disloyal to their king. That Christ was tempted proves the reality of His humanity, but it proves nothing more.

But if this be so, if our Lord's temptations all came upon Him from without; if there was no inward bias to evil in Him, as there is in us, to which the external solicitation to sin might appeal, then it may be said — and this is the last difficulty we shall consider in this chapter — that Christ's temptations were, after all, unlike ours, and that the graver half of their reality and terror is at once taken away. But is it so? Is the existence of a prior inclination to evil, or in other words, is a corrupt heart necessary to the gravity and reality of temptation? If so, how was the first Adam tempted? There was no bias to sin in him to which the tempter might appeal, and yet he fell; fell where Christ conquered. The difference, great and serious as it is, between Christ's temptations and our temptations, only makes His temptation the more like the temptation of Adam. The first and the second Adam were each typically attacked by the tempter, but where Adam yielded Christ overcame; and His victory — the victory of the new Head and Representative of Humanity — rolled back the shame and dishonor of our first parents' fall. Nay, more! An inward bias to evil is not even essential in our own case to the reality of temptation. Temptation may appeal to what is noblest and best, as well as to what is lowest and basest in us, and some of our sharpest and deadliest temptations arise, not from the inducement to commit open and flagrant transgression,

---

[6] Matthew 4:1; Mark 1:13; Luke 4:1

but from the subtle suggestions which come to us so often in our highest and best moments to do wrong for the sake of right, to satisfy lawful appetites by unlawful means, to serve the truth by a lie. The reality of Christ's temptations remains unbroken, although there was no sin in Him to which temptation might appeal.

Assuming, then, their reality, it will be well for us to consider some of the practical results which flow from this admission.

First of all, it is manifest, as has already been observed, that the entire moral significance of the temptation to Christ is vitally affected by this admission. If the temptation of Christ were only an act, however stately and solemn, in a great drama, the issues of which had been determined beforehand, and were wholly independent of its chief actors; if from the outset there was no real possibility of Christ yielding, had He chosen, to the tempter, then the majestic glory of Christ's victory over Satan is gone forever. It is only as we feel His temptation was not "acting" at all, but an awful and tremendous struggle between the Captain of our salvation and the prince of darkness — a struggle which Christ waged at the cost of terrible suffering and exhaustion — that we feel the full moral sublimity of His character, Who, though spent and weary with the forty days' fast which had preceded this final assault of the devil, and notwithstanding His physical weakness and need, foiled one after another all the assaults of the tempter's power. Instead of the admission of the reality of the temptation detracting from the moral glory and greatness of Christ, it adds immeasurable grandeur to His human character, and fills us with a new sense of His unapproachable goodness and unswerving fidelity to His Father, Whose kingdom He thus founded among men in tears and conflict and pain. But the admission of the reality of the temptation of our Lord affects us as well as Him. It must have been comparatively easy for the first disciples, who saw our Lord's human life, who lived with Him from day to day, and learned from this companionship His humanity as well as His divinity, who heard, possibly from Christ's own lips, the story of His struggle with the tempter in the wilderness, to realize the intensity and depth of Christ's sympathy with them in their temptations. What was easy for the twelve may be difficult for us. We have never seen Christ hungering and thirsting, or weary and tempted; we no longer think of Him as "the man of sorrows and acquainted with grief," for He is now seated at "the right hand of God," and crowned with the glory and praise of Heaven; and the present majesty and exaltation of the glorified Christ actually make it hard for us to realize that though He is "highly exalted," yet on the throne of His glory He bears for us a Brother's heart, is still "touched with the feeling of our infirmities," and still remembers the days of His flesh, when He was "in all points tempted like as we are, yet without sin."

We must go back to the story of this temptation, and feel its reality, if we would revive within us the sense of the warmth and vividness of Christ's sympathy with His disciples in all their struggles with evil. Here is our Lord entering into the lowest conditions of our lot, suffering as we suffer from the assaults of evil, fighting as we have to fight against temptation to sin, proving for Himself how "narrow is the gate and straitened the way that leadeth unto life;" and surely if sympathy is born out of a common experience of suffering, we may be assured, not only that Christ will stand by us and help us in every struggle we have to wage against sin, but that He enters into the bitterness of the struggle, and understands, better than even we ourselves do——

"How hard it is to be a Christian."

The reality of Christ's temptation is the one abiding pledge we possess at once of His deep and tender sympathy with us in every effort to resist evil, in every struggle to do right, and of His power and willingness to help "in time of need."

But it is more than this. It affects our feelings to Christ as well as our realization of His sympathy with us. No doubt it is possible to dwell too much on mere subjective emotion, and to lose the brightness and liberty of the Divine life in a too careful and constant scrutiny of our own affection to the Lord Jesus Christ. But if this be possible, it must not be forgotten that it is also possible to dwell too little on our feelings to Him, and to forget that He cares very much for the love and sympathy of His disciples for Himself. It is to be feared that the deep and reverent affection which the early disciples cherished for their Lord, the tender and constant sympathy with which they followed every movement of His earthly life, entering into its needs and sorrows and pains almost as if they were their own, are becoming rarer in the Church today, and that of other Churches than the Church at Ephesus He has to complain that "they have left their first love."[7] It may be that as we study His temptation, as we watch with Him through the long forty days of fasting and trial, as we gaze with reverence and love on the great conflict which closed the fast, and on the issues of which the salvation of the world was hanging, we may be led once more to cast around our Lord the arms of our poor sympathy and love, hardly knowing whether more to weep for the suffering He thus endured for us, or to rejoice in the matchless goodness which triumphed over the deadliest assaults of the tempter, and became the pledge of our final triumph as well.

---

[7] Revelation 2:4

"Then was Jesus led up of the Spirit into the wilderness to be tempted of the devil."

Matthew 4:1

"Straightway the Spirit driveth him forth into the wilderness: and he was in the wilderness forty days tempted of Satan."

Mark 1:12–13

"Jesus, full of the Holy Ghost, returned from the Jordan, and was led by the Spirit in the wilderness during forty days being tempted of the devil."

Luke 4:1

# III
## THE INSTRUMENT AND THE DIVINE ORDERING OF THE TEMPTATION

ALL the Evangelists who record the temptation of our Lord tell us expressly it was a temptation by "the devil." We have already remarked on the impossibility of accounting for temptation assaulting Christ unless some external and objective source of temptation be presupposed, and as in the special circumstances under which He was now placed He was removed from the possibility of temptation by man, the evangelic records are alike true to the facts of our Lord's position, and to the inherent necessity of the case, when they tell us that the temptation through which He was now to pass, arose from the malignity and subtlety of the devil.

To those who believe in the supernatural there will be no difficulty in the account which the Scriptures give — and nowhere more fully, or more explicitly, than in the teaching of the Lord Jesus Christ Himself — of the agency and power of the devil. That there are evil spirits as well as good spirits constantly surrounding man — the infranatural, if the word may be used, as well as the supernatural — that these spirits, in accordance with their nature, are banded together in rebellion against God, and in a ceaseless effort to overturn His kingdom; that they are under the leadership and control of a prince, or archdevil, of vast, although strictly limited power, and of infernal malignity and cunning, who is called "the Devil," "Satan," "Beelzebub," "the Prince of the Power of the Air," "the Prince of this world" — the two last expressions possibly summarizing the extent of the territory over which the power of the devil extends — that this evil spirit has usurped, and has been permitted by God provisionally to usurp, the government of this world, and to occupy the throne which belongs to God alone; that his sole object during the limited time of his dominion over men is to seduce them to join him in his revolt against the authority of God, and that for this purpose he approaches and assaults every human soul with an endless variety of seductions to evil, whence he derives the darkest and most terrible name given to him in Scripture of "the Tempter," is only the briefest summary of the teaching of the Bible on the agency and personality of the devil.

It is true that of late years doubts have arisen, not only amongst those who deny any authority to the Christian revelation, but also amongst some who accept its authority, as to whether there is any valid ground for assuming the existence of a personal devil. It has recently, for example, been gravely asked whether it would not be as well in future to spell the devil's name without the initial letter; and the recent outcry at the alteration by the Revisers of the New Testament of one petition in the Lord's Prayer from "Deliver us from evil" to "Deliver us from the evil one," was perhaps as much due to the theological implication of the alteration, as to a critical objection to the new translation itself; but in addition to the fact that any denial of the existence of a personal devil must necessarily be a denial of that of which, apart from Scripture, we can know nothing either way, it is difficult to see how such a denial can be reconciled with submission to the supreme authority of the Lord Jesus Christ. There has been an almost unanimous consent amongst all the profoundest theologians of the Christian Church on this point, and without therefore encumbering these pages with a discussion, which to be exhaustive would have to be too technical and theological for general readers, we shall assume what is generally understood by the personality of the devil, and we have now to consider the relation the temptation of our Lord bears to the devil as its instrument and cause.

In the previous chapters we have dwelt on the reality and the significance of the temptation to Christ Himself, and these have been

# THE INSTRUMENT AND THE DIVINE ORDERING OF THE TEMPTATION  25

the aspect in which both theology and the pulpit have commonly regarded it, but it has been too much forgotten that real as the temptation was to Christ, it was just as real to the devil himself. In point of fact the relation and significance of the temptation to the devil have hardly been so much as raised, and yet on the right apprehension of the meaning and motive of the devil in the temptation of Christ, depends very much of the reality of the temptation to Christ Himself.

Christ had become Incarnate to redeem the world from sin, and to restore the authority of God over a revolted race. His whole mission was summed up in the words of St. John, "To this end was the Son of God manifested, that He might destroy the works of the devil."[1] That He might overturn the kingdom of Satan, and reinstate the kingdom of God among men, might reveal at once the greatness of the sin of man, and the greatness of the glory which had been lost to him through his sin, might make it possible to man to recover this glory once more, Christ did not hesitate to abandon the infinite bliss and glory of Heaven, and to enter on a life filled with sorrow, and ending in the shame and darkness of the Cross. Is it to be wondered at, then, if he who had seduced man from his allegiance to God, whose infernal kingdom had been set up in the world on the ruins of the kingdom of God, who for long ages had been "the prince of this world," knowing the full significance of the advent of Christ, should rouse himself at the very outset of Christ's mission for a desperate struggle with the Prince of glory, Whose victory meant the destruction both of Satan and of his kingdom?

It is not a little remarkable that we find similar, if more limited, outbursts of the hostility and power of Satan at each of the great historical crises of the kingdom of God among men. Any special manifestation of the love and power of God in the gradual unfolding of the mystery of Redemption has always provoked a correspondent manifestation of the hatred of the devil both to God and to man. When Adam appears in Paradise — the first subject of the new kingdom of God on earth the devil appears too, and at once begins to tempt him

---

[1] 1 John 3:8

to his ruin.[2] When Israel is delivered from Egypt, and the first great step is taken of the founding of the Theocracy on earth, then again, according to Jewish tradition, Satan appears in the wilderness and seduces Israel by the worship of the golden calf.[3] When the worship of God is once more restored to the people of God after the exile, Satan appears hindering its re-institution, apparently suggesting that as Israel had been rejected by God the priesthood could never again be renewed.[4] When Christ is born "who is to rule all the nations," again we read, "there was war in heaven: Michael and his angels going forth to war with the dragon; and the dragon warred and his angels:"[5] the birth of our Lord being the signal for a furious outbreak of Satanic malignity and power. During the whole of Christ's earthly life that mysterious revelation of the same power, which the New Testament calls 'possession by devils,' occurs again and again. When Christ's kingdom is finally set up among men in the Church of the living God, Satan again appears, "and working with all power and signs and lying wonders," and "with all deceit of unrighteousness,"[6] he enters the Church, falsifying the Gospel, falsifying the worship of God, falsifying the kingdom of God, with lying prophecy, a lying priesthood, and a lying kingship, all of which unite against the office and the kingdom of Christ. According to the Apocalypse Satan's fury increases with his losses, and it finally culminates in that last and desperate assault on the kingdom of God — as if he hoped, even at the moment of the triumph of the kingdom, to wreck it forever — described in the mysterious words, "When the thousand years are finished, Satan shall be loosed out of his prison, and shall come forth to deceive the nations... and they went up over the breadth of the earth, and compassed the camp of the saints about, and the beloved city."[7]

Is it wonderful, we ask again, now the supreme moment in the

---

[2] Genesis 3
[3] Compare with Exodus 32.
[4] Zechariah 3:1–2
[5] Revelation 7:7
[6] Thessalonians 2:9–10
[7] Revelation 20:7–9

## THE INSTRUMENT AND THE DIVINE ORDERING OF THE TEMPTATION  27

history of the race has come, and the Deliverer of man from the power of the devil is about to begin His mighty work, that Satan should gird himself for a tremendous and deadly struggle with the Redeemer of the world? As Christ begins His Divine mission Satan arises to overturn it. The temptation is an attempt, almost majestic in its infernal daring, to assault the Son of God before His work had fully begun; to destroy the kingdom by conquering its King.

And here, it may be said in passing, we have another evidence of the reality of the temptation to our Lord. Satan was not playing at fighting. He would never have entered on the awful and perilous work of tempting Christ, if he had known from the outset his attack was doomed to failure.[8] As the reality of our Lord's manhood guaranteed on His side the reality of the temptation, so the reality of the struggle to Satan also guarantees from his side its reality to Christ. Instead of the temptation being an unreal encounter between the devil and Christ, it may be said without exaggeration that never has there been any encounter between the devil and a human soul so real, or on the results of which such vast and tremendous issues were depending. The redemption of the world, the final victory of good over evil, the glory of God Himself, were involved in the victory of Christ over the devil.

It is not necessary, as has sometimes been asserted, to the reality of the temptation, to suppose there must have been a bodily and visible appearance of Satan to Christ. For not only have we no authority in the New Testament to warrant us in believing that Satan has the power to make himself visible at will, but if the visibility of the tempter is essential to the temptation, then it is certain none of us can be tempted by the devil. The truth is, as we shall see in a moment, that so far from a personal and bodily manifestation of the tempter being a necessary part of temptation, it is rather a hindrance to its reality and intensity than otherwise. There is, moreover, not a word in any one of the three narratives of the temptation of Christ which would warrant the belief that the devil became personally visible to Christ. Indeed, one of the temptations, and perhaps the keenest and deadliest of the

---

[8] We may assume that so much as this Satan must have known, although, doubtless, the popular conception of the practical "omniscience" of Satan has no foundation in Scripture.

three, must necessarily have been visionary and subjective, for no one can imagine that there was any high mountain from the summit of which Christ could be shown "all the kingdoms of the world;" or that if there was an elevation sufficiently high for such an impossible view, Christ could have seen, with His bodily eyes, such a prospect "in a moment of time," and if this temptation was mental and subjective without losing its reality, the rest of the temptations may have equally well been so too. Further, it may be urged, and with very considerable force, that the distinct assertion of Scripture that Christ "was *in all points* tempted like as we are," precludes the supposition of any visible appearance of Satan to Christ.

The safest way of discussing the specific mode in which the devil approached Christ is to leave it in the vague and indefinite terms in which Scripture leaves it. "The tempter came ... unto Him"[9] is all we are told, and yet vague and indefinite as the expression may be, it is full of suggestion because of its vagueness. Is it not so with all our own temptations? Can we say, on looking back on them, more than this, that in some way, we knew not how, "the tempter came" to us? How the tempter gains access to our own hearts, how he draws back one by one the bolts which bar his entrance there, how he creeps along the secret avenues of the soul, how the dark shadow falls on the chambers of imagery within, how he reaches the spring and fountain of life, the heart itself, and poisons it with evil; how he intermingles his foul and dark suggestions with our own thoughts, filling the soul with all disgusting and loathsome shapes and forms of sin; how, at last, he lays his hand on the citadel of the soul, the will itself, and slowly and surely leads it toward the evil from which it had struggled to be free, until his infernal work is done, and — O hideous mystery! — these unclean desires seem to be rising from our own hearts, these dark imaginations to be our own foul thoughts within, and these secret inclinations to yield to temptation seem to be our own will bending and swaying toward sin, and at length the voice of conscience is silenced, and "lust hath conceived and brought forth sin;" — how

---

[9] Matthew 4:3

## THE INSTRUMENT AND THE DIVINE ORDERING OF THE TEMPTATION 29

all this can be we cannot tell; we only know it is so. The process and the mode of temptation may be a mystery, but its pain and peril are nonetheless real. We, too, can only say, "the tempter came unto us."

But it is not enough to speak of the temptation of our Lord as if the devil were solely responsible for it, and there was no Divine ordering to be seen in the conflict between the prince of darkness and the Savior of the world. It is a remarkable fact that each of the three evangelists who record the temptation uses a different, and yet most significant expression to denote the Divine appointment of the temptation of Christ. St. Matthew says, "Then was Jesus *led up* of the Spirit into the wilderness to be tempted of the devil,"[10] the gracious but effectual conduct of the Savior by the Spirit to the temptation being implied in the word used:[11] St. Luke says,[12] "And Jesus, full of the Holy Spirit, returned from the Jordan, and was *led* by the Spirit in the wilderness during forty days, being tempted of the devil;" the Spirit — for this seems the meaning of the word here used[13] — inspiring the journey to the desert and to the temptation that awaited Christ there; while St. Mark with characteristic energy of expression compresses into its most vigorous form[14] the Divine ordering and purpose of the temptation; "Straightway," he says, "the Spirit driveth him forth into the wilderness. And He was in the wilderness forty days tempted of Satan."[15]

The devil was the instrument of the temptation, but God ordained it.

And this distinction between the agent and the ordainer of temptation is not one of words. For not only does the withdrawal of anything, save positive sin, from the sphere of God's will, affect the integrity of His moral government of the race, and relax the hold which God has on the progress of human affairs, but the teaching of Scripture is only

---

[10] Matthew 4:1
[11] ἀνήχθη.
[12] Luke 4:1
[13] ἤγετο.
[14] ἐκβάλλει.
[15] Mark 1:12

to be reconciled with itself by bearing in mind that God may ordain a moral discipline for the soul, of which it is impossible He should be the instrument and immediate cause. We are told, for example, by St. James,[16] "Let no man say when he is tempted, I am tempted of God: for God cannot be tempted with evil, and He Himself tempteth no man," and yet we are equally told, "It came to pass after these things that God did tempt Abraham;"[17] and if it be said that this only means that God did try Abraham, the difficulty is removed but a step farther back, for trial is always temptation, just as temptation is always trial. The true solution of the apparent contradiction seems to be suggested by the typical temptation of Christ, that while God Himself never does offer, and never can offer personal seduction or inducement to sin to the soul — the supposition itself is utterly blasphemous — yet God may permit, and may will, that the soul should pass through temptation as the only means of that purifying and strengthening discipline to which we referred in the first chapter, as the chief object and result of all moral trial of every kind. And hence it is that the same temptation may be said, from one point of view, to come from God, and from another, to come from the devil. Thus, to take perhaps the most striking illustration of this truth to be found in Scripture, the numbering of the people by David is said in the Book of Samuel to have been the result of God "moving" David "against" Israel;[18] while in the parallel history of the Book of Chronicles we read, "And Satan stood up against Israel and provoked David to number Israel."[19] Of course there is an absolute opposition between the ends which God has in view and those the devil compasses in the temptation of men. God ordains our temptation in order to purify us as gold is purified in the fire. The devil tempts us to destroy us as rotten wood is consumed in the furnace. God leads us into temptation in order to bless and to crown us with the reward of the victory. The devil tempts us to curse

[16] James 1:13
[17] Genesis 12:1
[18] 2 Samuel 24:1
[19] 1 Chronicles 21:1

# THE INSTRUMENT AND THE DIVINE ORDERING OF THE TEMPTATION

us with the shame and the guilt of defeat. God tempts to save; Satan tempts to destroy.

And this double aspect of temptation may suggest to us, in conclusion, some of the practical lessons which even thus early we may learn for ourselves from the temptation of Christ.

**1.** We may learn that it is never the will of God that we should voluntarily enter into temptation.

Christ did not. He was, as we have seen, "led" of the Spirit, "driven" by the Spirit into the wilderness, and because He was, and did not go there of His own accord, He found power to overcome. And so is it with us. It is possible, alas! for us to encounter temptations which God never meant us to face; to enter into temptation of our own self-will; to enter it therefore without God; to put ourselves in the way of evil; to go as near to sin as we think we dare without touching it; but if we do thus "tempt God" we have no right to wonder if He seems to desert us in our hour of sorest need. It is we who have really deserted Him by "entering" into temptation; and our peril is the direct punishment and result of our own perversity and sin. Whatever blessings may result to the soul from "enduring temptation" they come only to them who do not "go," but are "led" by the Spirit into the peril and the fight.

**2.** But we may go farther than this. Not only ought we never to enter temptation of ourselves, but we may pray, and we ought to pray, that God would not "bring us" into it.

When we think of our own weakness, of how little we can trust ourselves, of how much may be involved in a single struggle, or a single defeat, there is, perhaps, no petition in the "Lord's Prayer" which comes more nearly home to us than this — "Bring us not into temptation,"[20] and to pray it is the sign, not of cowardice, but of courage; not of weakness, but of strength; for it is the courage and strength of those who have learned the lesson, "Let him that thinketh he standeth take heed lest he fall."[21]

**3.** But, should God lead us, as He led Christ, into temptation, then we may confidently appeal to God for grace to overcome.

---

[20] Matthew 6:13
[21] 1 Corinthians 10:12

Hard and desperate as the fight may be, if only we are true to God, we shall overcome at last And yet not we, for God will fight for us and with us. "The battle is the Lord's," not ours, and He who led us into peril will Himself furnish us with all the strength for the battle which we may need, and finally bring us scatheless from the fight singing, "Now unto Him that is able to guard us from stumbling, and to set us before the presence of His glory, without blemish, in exceeding joy, to the only God our Savior, through Jesus Christ our Lord, be glory, majesty, dominion and power, before all time, and now, and for evermore." Amen.[22]

---

[22] Jude 24, 25

"Then cometh Jesus from Galilee to the Jordan unto John, to be baptized of him. But John would have hindered him, saying, I have need to be baptized of thee, and comest thou to me? But Jesus answering said unto him, Suffer it now: for thus it becometh us to fulfil all righteousness. Then he suffereth him. And Jesus, when he was baptized, went up straightway from the water: and lo, the heavens were opened unto him, and he saw the Spirit of God descending as a dove, and coming upon him; and lo, a voice out of the heavens, saying, This is my beloved Son, in whom I am well pleased.

"Then was Jesus led up of the Spirit into the wilderness to be tempted of the devil. And when he had fasted forty days and forty nights, he afterward hungered."

Matthew 3:13–17; 4:1–2

"And it came to pass in those days, that Jesus came from Nazareth of Galilee, and was baptized of John in the Jordan. And straight way coming up out of the water, he saw the heavens rent asunder, and the Spirit as a dove descending upon him; and a voice came out of the heavens, Thou art my beloved Son, in Thee I am well pleased. And straightway the Spirit driveth him forth into the wilderness."

Mark 1:9–12

"Now it came to pass, when all the people were baptized, that, Jesus also having been baptized, and praying, the heaven was opened, and the Holy Ghost descended in a bodily form, as a dove, upon him, and a voice came out of heaven, Thou art my beloved Son; in Thee I am well pleased.

"And Jesus, full of the Holy Spirit, returned from the Jordan, and was led by the Spirit in the wilderness during forty days, being tempted of the devil. And he did eat nothing in those days: and when they were completed, he hungered."

Luke 3:21–22; 4:1–2

# IV

## THE TIME AND PLACE OF THE TEMPTATION

EACH of the three evangelists who record the temptation of our Lord begins the record with a word which indicates the close and profound connection there was between the temptation and the events which immediately preceded it in the life of Christ. St. Matthew commences his account with the word "Then;" and St. Mark and St. Luke do not even interrupt their narrative, but as if the temptation were only a part of what had just gone before, they couple its record with that of the preceding history by the conjunction "And." Now to say that Christ's temptation was not an isolated event in His experience, wholly disconnected with His previous history, is only to say of our Lord what is true of every temptation that assaults the human soul. The temptations of today are always more or less the result of the life of yesterday, the character and actions of the past reappearing, not only in the good, but in the evil of the present. For even where there has been no yielding to sin, as in the case of our Lord, it by no means follows, as we shall see, that the triumphs of goodness itself may not be used by the tempter as fresh occasions of temptation to the soul. It is from the loftiest heights of holiness that the deepest fall into sin is always possible.

To understand fully the temptation of Christ, we must therefore understand the period in His human life at which it took place, and the history which immediately preceded it.

One great event — the Baptism of Christ — stands out in the

sacred narrative in each of the three evangelists as having been the immediate precursor of the temptation; and we have now to inquire into the significance of our Lord's baptism, and into its relation to the temptation that succeeded it.

The baptism of Christ was, first of all, the public announcement and inauguration of Christ to His work. John the Baptist had come "to bear witness of the Light that all might believe through him,"[1] and now his work was nearly done. He had "prepared the way of the Lord" by preaching "repentance unto Israel," and by warning men everywhere that One greater than himself was at hand. One last act — and it was John's greatest act — remained to be done, the solemn setting apart of the Christ to His redeeming work. At length the time for this had come. Jesus was baptized of John in the Jordan. The baptism closed our Lord's private life, and began His public ministry. He who had gone down into the water known to men as "the Son of Mary," came up thence declared to be "the Son of God." The baptism, with the opened heavens, and the Spirit "descending like a dove," and "abiding" on Jesus, and the witness borne by the voice of God Himself, "This is My beloved Son in whom I am well pleased," was the sublime inauguration of the Savior of the world to His great mission. From that hour John's prophetic work was done. It expired, to use Davison's beautiful image, as Old Testament prophecy had expired, with "the Gospel upon its tongue."[2] As soon as the Christ was manifested unto Israel, John begins to vanish from the history; as "the star which opes the gates of day, and shuts in the night" is never found very far from the sun, and as the sun appears is lost in its light, so John passes out of sight as Christ draws near. He had but one more word to speak — and with that his witness to Christ was ended — "Behold the Lamb of God which taketh away the sin of the world."[3]

"Then," we read, as immediately following the baptism, "was Jesus led up of the Spirit into the wilderness to be tempted of the devil." We may see, in part, at any rate, the reason of the temptation thus coming

---

[1] John 1:7
[2] Davison, John (1870). *Discourses on Prophecy* (p. 253).
[3] John 1:29

## THE TIME AND PLACE OF THE TEMPTATION

after the baptism. As the baptism had announced the Christ for His work, so the temptation now announces the work to the Christ. Christ's first public act, His first step in His ministry of redemption, is to be tempted by the devil. He had come to "destroy the works of the devil," and here, in the wilderness, He enters on the first great act of the struggle. Christ and Satan meet face to face. The beginning of the work is at once the key to the whole, and the prophecy of its end.

How far our Lord Himself may have learned from His temptation the nature of the great work to accomplish which He had become incarnate, we do not know. The whole subject of the growth of Christ's human soul, the steps by which it grew into the full consciousness of His Divine mission, is so obscure and mysterious, that it is better not to speculate in a region which the wisdom of Scripture has left in darkness; but we can scarcely be wrong in supposing that if the baptism of Jesus first fully revealed to Him the full glory of His Person, and of His relation to the Eternal Father — a glory which had been slowly dawning on Him from His youth upward — so the temptation first fully set before Him the greatness of the struggle He had undertaken to endure, and the full bitterness of the cup which His Father had given Him to drink. The two together, the baptism and the temptation, complete the solemn announcement of the Savior for His work. The inauguration is followed by the initiation. The commissioning, if we may use the term with deepest reverence, of the Captain of our salvation, is succeeded by His first great conflict with the prince of this world. Christ's work has begun.

But the baptism of our Lord did more than precede His temptation; it prepared the way for it, and this in two ways: it prepared Christ for the temptation, and it prepared the temptation for Christ.

It prepared Christ, first, for His temptation. We have already noticed, in another connection, that the Evangelists who record the temptation emphasize with marked significance the fact that Jesus was "led" or "driven" *of the Spirit* to His temptation. But St. Luke adds to this a still more pregnant expression, for he tells us that Jesus, *"full of the Holy Ghost*, returned from the Jordan, and was led by the Spirit in the wilderness during forty days, being tempted of the devil."[4] That this fullness of the Holy Ghost had come upon our Lord's human nature at His baptism, the Scripture record seems plainly to declare, and if so we can see at once how closely it was connected with the temptation that followed it. The Divine equipment of the man Christ Jesus preceded the long struggle in which He was now to engage. In all things our example, He puts on "the whole armor of God" before entering on "the good fight of faith."

There is another and an analogous preparation for coming conflict bestowed on Christ at a later period of His ministry, and which serves to illustrate the special meaning of the baptism in the light in which we are now considering it. Once, and only once, again in the earthly life of our Lord do we read of the voice from heaven uttering the same glorious and solemn witness to the Divine Sonship and mission of Jesus which was given at His baptism. At the transfiguration of Christ, a second time was heaven opened, and a second time God Himself bore witness to His Son in the words, "This is My beloved Son in whom I am well pleased, hear ye Him."[5] But what followed the transfiguration and the heavenly witness? The passion came after the transfiguration, just as the temptation came after the baptism; the glory of the "holy mount " being the preparation of Christ for His cross, just as the fullness of the Holy Ghost received at His baptism was the Divine preparation for the conflict with the devil in the wilderness.

But the baptism had a further and final relation to the temptation. If it prepared Christ for the temptation, it also prepared the temptation for Christ. The baptism of the Holy Ghost was not accidentally followed by the first assault of the tempter on Jesus.

It is true that we are apt to think that the possession of unusual spiritual power, or the consciousness of peculiar spiritual elevation, is enough to secure the soul from any further assaults of evil; and that the loftiest elevations of the spiritual life must necessarily be the freest from spiritual peril. But it is not so really. In this life, and

---

[4] Luke 4:1
[5] Matthew 17:5, and the parallel passages.

we speak of this life alone when we speak of temptation, moments of spiritual exaltation and rapture are sure to be succeeded by some terrible and searching temptation. It is not merely that seasons of peculiar blessedness, whether in spiritual or in temporal things, need to be proved and chastened by the keen and terrible fires of trial; but the trial itself oftentimes arises from the very blessedness we enjoy. It was when Abraham's heart was filled with joy at the fulfillment of the long-delayed promise God had made to him, and Isaac was growing from boyhood into manhood, every year bringing nearer and nearer the rich heritage of blessing which rested on the heir of the promise, that we come across the ominous words, "It came to pass after these things, God did tempt Abraham."[6] It was when David had reached the zenith of his prosperity and power, and the glory of his house seemed established forever, that his great temptation came upon him, and he fell.[7] It was when Simon Peter had been so filled with the overwhelming sense of his Master's grace and love that he had declared, "Even if I must die with Thee, yet I will not deny Thee,"[8] that the hour of his proving, and his bitter failure in the denial of Christ, drew near. It was when St. Paul had been "caught up into the third heaven," and had heard "unspeakable words, which it is not lawful for a man to utter," that there was given to him "a thorn in the flesh, a messenger of Satan to buffet him, that he should not be exalted overmuch."[9] And it was when Jesus was "full of the Holy Ghost," the Spirit having descended and remaining on Him, that "immediately the Spirit driveth Him forth into the wilderness, and He was in the wilderness forty days, tempted of Satan."

And so it always is. When we are walking softly with God, and there is not much light about the path, and we rejoice, if we rejoice at all, "with trembling," we are comparatively safe from the tempter: but when we walk on the heights above, and stand in the sunlight of heaven, and the heart beats high with exalting raptures, danger is

---

[6] Genesis 22:1
[7] 2 Samuel 11
[8] Matthew 26:34
[9] 2 Corinthians 12:7

near. Close to those sunlit heights there yawn downward at our feet black and awful precipices, and one false step may be fatal. Hours of solitude and of depression and of self-distrust are not our most perilous hours; it is when all heaven seems opened above us, and God to be very near to us, and His Spirit to be filling us with peace and joy, that we most need to watch and pray. The wilderness with its fierce temptation always comes near to the baptism with its heavenly vision; and from the conflict of the perfect man with the tempter the voice sounds afresh in our ears, "Let him that thinketh he standeth take heed lest he fall."[10]

And now let us turn to the consideration of the place in which the temptation occurred.

The only account given to us of the locality of the temptation is that it took place in "the wilderness," but where this wilderness was situated we do not know. It is true that there is a spot near to Jericho which has long been pointed out as the traditional locality of the temptation, and which has taken its name (The Quarantania)[11] from the forty days' fast in the wilderness, but there is no evidence whatsoever for the tradition, and the utmost that can be said in its favor is that the place is not unsuited to the solitary and awful conflict of our Lord with the tempter. A high and conical mountain, rising out of a lifeless and joyless desert plain, and looking over the waters of the Dead Sea, the sides of the mountain pierced with innumerable caves (which were once tenanted by hermits), and terminating in precipices on every side, is the traditional locality which has been identified with "the wilderness" of the Gospel history. But whether this were the true locality of the temptation, or whether, as for some reasons seem more probable, the Desert of Sinai was the scene of the conflict, there are lessons to be learned from the nature of the locality itself, which are independent of its exact position.

It was, first of all, manifestly a place of absolute solitude.

We referred on a previous page to the fullness of the Holy Ghost which was bestowed on our Lord at His baptism, and to the revelation

---

[10] 1 Corinthians 10:12
[11] Also known as The Mount of Temptation.

## THE TIME AND PLACE OF THE TEMPTATION    41

which in all probability this fullness of the Spirit gave to His human soul of the nature and glory of His Divine mission in the world.

But if this were so, and if, as we believe, Jesus was "made in all points like as we are, yet without sin," solitude even apart from temptation would become a necessity to Christ after such a revelation. He would be led by the instincts and necessities of His own spiritual life to yearn for solitude that he might ponder the vast and glorious work on which He had entered at His baptism by John. It seems, indeed, as if all the noblest and most distinguished servants of God had been forbidden to begin their great work until they had passed through the discipline and strengthening of some such period of solitude and fellowship with God. Moses spent forty years in the silence of the desert before he was called by God to be the leader and lawgiver of Israel.[12] Elijah was alone with God for forty days and forty nights on Mount Horeb before coming forth to his final conflict with the priests of Baal, and with an idolatrous king, and an idolatrous people.[13] St. Paul tells us that after it had pleased God to "reveal His Son in me," "immediately I conferred not with flesh and blood," "but I went away into Arabia,"[14] and there is little, if any, doubt that the "Arabia" into which he retired was the same desert of Sinai where Moses had received the law and Elijah had heard "the still, small voice" of God. "Standing," to quote the words of the Bishop of Durham,[15] "on the threshold of the new Covenant, he was anxious to look upon the birthplace of the old: that dwelling for a while in seclusion in the presence of 'the mount that burned with fire,' he might ponder over the transient glories of the ministration of death and apprehend its real purpose in relation to the more glorious covenant which was now to supplant it. Here, surrounded by the children of the desert, the descendants of Hagar[16] the bondswoman, he read the true meaning and power of the law. In the rugged and barren region whence it issued he saw a

---

[12] Acts 7:30
[13] 1 Kings 19:8
[14] Galatians 1:16–17
[15] Lightfoot, Joseph Barber (1880). *St. Paul's Epistle to the Galatians* (p. 88).
[16] An Egyptian handmaid of Sarai (Sarah), who gave her to Abraham to bear a child. The product of the union was Abraham's firstborn, Ishmael.

fit type of that bleak desolation which it created and was intended to create in the soul of man." It may well have been to this same desert, already consecrated by the most sacred memories——

> "Where all around, on mountain, sand, and sky,
> God's chariot wheels have left distinctest trace,"

that One infinitely greater than either Moses or Elias — and to whom their homage on the Mount of Transfiguration testified that both law and prophets bowed before the supreme authority and glory of the Christ — was led, that amidst its awful solitudes and surrounded by its sacred memories, He might meditate on the nature and the issues of that redeeming work which He had just begun, and to accomplish, which He had come into the world.

But if this solitude of the desert afforded to Christ a lengthened season for meditation on His great work, and for fellowship with His Father, we must not forget that it also deepened and aggravated the severity of the conflict which our Lord endured from the assault of the tempter. We know from our own experience the helpfulness of a human voice and a human heart by our side in times of the deepest spiritual darkness and trial: we know how even the simple entreaty by those we love, not to give way to temptation, often girds us with new strength, and decides the wavering will; and because Christ was in very deed our brother, "the Son of Man," He too must have felt the inspiration and the courage which human sympathy and human goodness afford to those who are sore beset of the devil. In another great crisis of our Lord's life, the temptation which fell on Him in the Garden of Gethsemane, and of which He Himself spoke as "the prince of this world coming"[17] to Him, He besought the three of His disciples whom He most trusted to "watch with him,"[18] as if He longed to feel the comfort and help of their companionship in His awful agony; but He asked, it may be added, in vain. The second temptation, like the first, was to be endured alone. Gethsemane was as truly a solitude to

---

[17] John 14:30
[18] Matthew 26:38

Christ as the wilderness. And in this, the first temptation of Christ, as in the second, He is withdrawn from all human companionship, and from the sound of human voices, and the touch of human love, that alone He may face the tempter, and in the dread conflict be cast on His God alone. How immeasurably this solitude added to the anguish and bitterness of the conflict we can only faintly imagine; that it left a dread of the same solitude occurring again we may see, not only from the pathetic appeal of which we have just spoken, which Jesus made to His disciples in the garden of Gethsemane, to "watch with Him," but from the sad remonstrance He addressed to His disciples concerning their desertion of Him in His hour of need, "The hour cometh, yea is come, that ye shall leave Me alone, and yet I am not alone, because the Father is with Me."[19]

But another purpose than that of solitude was secured by the wilderness being selected as the scene of Christ's temptation; it necessitated the long period of fasting which preceded the final temptation. "In those days" — and St. Luke is referring to the forty days of the sojourn in the desert — "He did eat nothing;"[20] and in St. Matthew we read, "When He had fasted forty days and forty nights He afterwards hungered."[21] Now this fast had a double significance, first in regard to the relation Christ bore to the Jewish law, and then in relation to our Lord Himself.

Twice, and only twice before, is a fast similar to Christ's recorded in the history of the Bible, and it is not a little significant that in both cases the fast took place in the wilderness, and in both cases it was a fast of the two great typical precursors of our Lord in the Jewish Church. Moses, the giver of the law, and who declared to the people, "The Lord thy God will raise up unto thee a Prophet from the midst of thee, of thy brethren, like unto me; unto Him shall ye hearken,"[22] had fasted in the wilderness forty days and forty nights;[23] and Elijah,

---

[19] John 16:32
[20] Luke 4:2
[21] Matthew 4:2
[22] Deuteronomy 18:15
[23] Exodus 24:18

the typical prophet of the Old Covenant, had also fasted for the same time in the same desert.[24] The first public act of the ministry of our Lord declares he has not come to "destroy, but to fulfill the law." By one significant act He binds Himself to the old at the very moment of inaugurating the new.

But the fast had its special relation to Christ's spiritual equipment for the conflict through which He was now to pass. In every age of the Church's history, and in almost every religion on the face of the earth, the practice of fasting has been the witness to the supremacy of the higher over the lower nature in man, and to the victory which may be gained by the spirit over the affections and passions of the flesh. Christ Himself bore witness to the value of this discipline of the body by His fast in the wilderness. About to enter on His great work, and to encounter the fiery darts of the devil, He equips Himself alike for the work and for the conflict, by a long and deliberate subordination of His bodily to His spiritual nature, by the assertion of the utter insignificance of the demands of the flesh as compared with the deeper necessities of the spirit He Himself is the great illustration of the meaning of His own words, "If any man would come after Me, let him deny himself and take up his cross daily and follow Me."[25]

No doubt it is easy to say that even fasting has been abused, and has been made a foe rather than a friend to the spiritual life. When the subordination of the lower to the higher nature, which alone gives all its moral value to fasting, has been lost sight of; when fasting has been practiced for its own sake, rather than as a means to an end higher than itself; when instead of taking its place as one of the conditions of spiritual endowment for any special spiritual work, it has been made a counsel of perfection, and exalted into a good in itself, then fasting has lost its moral worth, and a protest against the fast may be really a higher moral act than the fast itself.

But in the present day, and amid the growing luxuriousness of the age in which we live, it is possible that we may be in danger of forgetting that fasting has still its legitimate place in the culture of the

---

[24] 1 Kings 19:8
[25] Luke 9:23

spiritual life, and that there is a true as well as a false asceticism in the kingdom of God. The form which the denial of the lower nature may take is comparatively unimportant; whether we abstain literally for a time from our wonted food and drink, or whether we refuse to gratify any of the sinless desires of which every human life is full, matters but little so long as the moral significance of the self-denial is reached in the resolute subordination of the lower and fleshly nature to the higher, even at the cost of pain, and suffering, and the mortification of the flesh. If an apostle could say, "I buffet my body and bring it into bondage, lest by any means, after that I have preached to others, I myself should be rejected,"[26] how little can any of us afford to neglect that bodily discipline, that gymnastic of the lower nature, which St. Paul tells is "profitable for a little,"[27] and the disregard of which has so often brought decay and death on the nobler life of the soul. High achievements in duty, continual victories over temptation and sin, the mastery of "the flesh" which besets us all, and without whose repression the spiritual life itself becomes enervated and luxurious, are not to be gained without much personal self-denial and pain, and without a daily self-discipline of which fasting ought to form at least a subordinate part.

One further point, moreover, in the locality chosen for the temptation remains to be noticed. St. Mark alone preserves for us the graphic touch in the picture, "He was with the wild beasts."[28] It is difficult, perhaps, to put into words all the subtle suggestions of this pregnant phrase — the imagination is often a better interpreter of Scripture than the logical reason — but some glimpses at any rate of its meaning may be caught. Adam lost his regal control and dominion over the lower animals by his fall: Christ regained it by His victory. The crown of man's lordship over the brute creation which had been lost by the first Adam is restored by the second. Adam turned Paradise into a desert by his sin: Jesus turns the desert into Paradise by His victory over sin and the wild beasts; and it adds inexpressible pathos to our

---

[26] 1 Corinthians 9:27
[27] 1 Timothy 4:8
[28] Mark 1:13

Lord's temptation if we think of Him not only as confronted by the great enemy — that adversary whom Scripture itself compares to a "roaring lion walking about seeking whom he may devour"[29] — but as surrounded by a fierce and bloodthirsty crew of wild beasts of prey, each one intent on His destruction, as eager for His blood as the devil was for His soul, but kept in terror, and subdued by the majesty and might of Him who had come to regain that lordship of man over the creation, which at the beginning was "put into subjection under his feet," but which had been forfeited by the fall.

What deeper meanings there may be in this mysterious phrase, "He was with the wild beasts," we may never on earth fully know. We only know that for ourselves temptation is often nothing but the assault of what has been called "the wild beast in every man" on that which is best and holiest in the soul, and although in the pure and perfect soul of Jesus there never was aught but what was divine and gentle and good, yet even He "made in all points like unto His brethren," may have been permitted to feel the assault of those seductions to evil which in us arise from our lower and evil nature, but which came to Him from the temptations of the devil from without. When He was tempted to make the stones into bread that He might satisfy the cravings of the hunger of the body, He passed through a temptation which is the pregnant type of all those temptations which come to us from "the flesh," and which gives a new meaning to the graphic words of St. Mark, "He was with the wild beasts."

And these were in the wilderness. Christ had left the haunts of men far behind, but he had not left temptation and danger behind. Driven by the Spirit into the desert, He finds the devil waiting for Him even there: and so we learn the last, and perhaps the most vital lesson the scene of the temptation was meant to teach us. In every age of the Church's history men and women have imagined that by fleeing from the world they could flee from temptation: and the "religious houses" of the Roman Catholic Church, its monasteries and convents, the cell of the anchorite or the recluse, and the pillow of the miserable

---

[29] 1 Peter 5:8

devotee, all have been hailed as retreats from the world, because they were believed to be refuges from temptation. How deadly the disaster that has come to the spiritual life of those who thus imagined they could serve God best by breaking God's own laws, it is needless to say; but against this foolish dream of escaping temptation by fleeing from the world, the temptation of Jesus in the wilderness is the divine and solemn warning. He found the devil in the deepest solitudes of the desert: and we shall find that he waits for us there too. To escape from temptation we must escape from life, for whether in the city or in the desert the tempter is near.

"And the tempter came and said unto him, If thou art the Son of God, command that these stones become bread. But he answered and said, It is written, Man shall not live by bread alone, but by every word that proceedeth out of the mouth of God."
Matthew 4:3–4

"And the devil said unto him, If thou art the Son of God, command this stone that it become bread. And Jesus answered unto him, It is written, Man shall not live by bread alone."
Luke 4:3–4

# V

# THE FIRST TEMPTATION

It is only in a very limited sense that we can speak of this temptation as being the first temptation of our Lord. It is true that it is the first of which we have any detailed record in the Gospels, but both St. Mark and St. Luke expressly state that the temptation of Christ had been going on incessantly throughout the forty days which preceded the final assault of the tempter. "He was in the wilderness forty days tempted of Satan,"[1] are the words of St. Mark, while St. Luke says, "Jesus... was led by the Spirit in the wilderness during forty days, being tempted of the devil."[2] The forty days of fasting were also forty days of temptation, culminating, as we shall now see, in three supreme and typical temptations, embodying in the ideal form in which they were presented to Christ all the temptations to which man is subject; the temptation, first of all, of the bodily or lower nature; then the temptation of the soul, or higher nature; and lastly, the temptation of the spiritual or highest part of man's nature. Or to put the same truth in another form, as there are three possible relations in which God stands to man, the relation of creation, or of providence, or of redemption, so these three final temptations of our Lord successively touch each one of these spheres of man's life; the first belonging to the lowest sphere, that of creation; the second to another and a higher sphere, that of providence; while the third and last reaches to the

---
[1] Mark 1:13
[2] Luke 4:2

loftiest of all the divine relations of human life, the sphere of the redemptive kingdom of God.

We have to consider now the meaning of the first temptation as it was presented to Christ.

For forty days and forty nights Jesus had eaten nothing. He had passed through a fast that recalled the great typical fasts of the Old Testament economy — passed through it that at least He might bear witness that in the new kingdom of God He was founding on earth, the lower nature of man was not less under the control of the higher than it was in the ancient kingdom of Judaism — but at the end of the forty days, when the cycle of the fast was complete, nature reasserted her claims. "When they were completed He hungered."[3]

Now, hunger is of all physical torments the most intolerable, with the single exception of the pangs of thirst, and even this latter misery we can hardly doubt was added to the Savior's suffering at the end of His fast; for although we are not told that He was enduring the pains of thirst as well as those of hunger, yet we may be sure that water was as little likely to have been found in the wilderness as bread. And it is this exhaustion and faintness of body which the devil uses as the instrument and occasion of the first temptation. We have already seen that there is no necessity to imagine any visible appearance of Satan to Christ, for the objective reality of temptation in no way depends on the personal manifestation of the tempter, and we may therefore, without irreverence, imagine the temptation as rising up within the soul of Christ, as our temptations arise within ourselves, as if it had sprung from the natural and lawful desires and necessities of His own bodily nature. 'I am weak, and faint, and hungry from my long fast and watching and conflict; why should I not at once satisfy the hunger of my body — hunger it is no sin for Me to feel, for it is only a consequence of that humanity I have taken upon Myself — by working a miracle and changing these stones which lie at My feet into bread?'

But the suggestion by the tempter to the mind of our Lord that He would do well to exert His miraculous power in order to satisfy

---

[3] Luke 4:2

the pangs of hunger does not, as it seems to us, reveal the deepest and most infernal subtlety of this first temptation. Both St. Matthew and St. Luke tell us that the temptation began with an appeal to Christ's divinity. "*If Thou be the Son of God*, command that these stones be made bread," and these words are profoundly significant. Immediately before Christ had gone up into the wilderness to be tempted of the devil, He had been baptized by John in the Jordan, and heaven had been opened, and the voice of God Himself had been heard declaring, "Thou art My beloved Son in whom I am well pleased." We have already endeavored to understand the meaning of the baptism in its relation to our Lord's own consciousness, and although the growth of the consciousness of the Divine nature in our Lord must be to us a dark, and possibly an insoluble mystery, yet as we have seen it seems not improbable that this heavenly voice gave to Jesus the first full assurance of His Divine mission, and that then there arose in Him in all its wonder and glory the consciousness, which from the first had been latent and slumbering in His soul, of His Divine relationship to God and of the work He had to fulfill in the world as the "beloved Son" in whom the Father was "well pleased."

This deep and blessed sense of Christ's filial relation to God Satan now uses as the lever of this first temptation. 'Thou art the Son of God; Thou hast heard the voice from heaven witnessing to Thy sonship; Thou hast all power given to Thee on earth; Thou hast a Divine mission to fulfill; why not test Thy power, and begin Thy mission now and here? Thou art hungry from fasting in Thy Father's work, command that these stones be made bread. If not, Thou mayest perish from hunger before Thy work has well begun, and Thy refusal may frustrate the end for which Thou hast come into the world.'

But even this account does not exhaust the full force of the temptation. It is impossible to overlook the dark suggestion implied in the first word of the tempter, "IF Thou be the Son of God," of doubt as to Christ's Divine Sonship, doubt which only a miraculous exertion of His power could answer and remove. 'If Thou be the Son of God, command that these stones be made bread; otherwise how shalt Thou know Thou art not self-deceived as to Thy Sonship and Thy mission? There is an "if," a terrible "if," before even Thine assurance of Thy Divine nature: destroy the doubt forever by one wonder-working word. Divine Sonship must mean Divine power; prove the Sonship by exerting the power. Thou hast done nothing with Thy Divine power for thirty long years; use it now. Use it for a holy and lawful end, and with the command that these stones be made bread — a command they shall hear and obey — at once satisfy Thy hunger, and forever verify Thy Divine mission among men.'

Such, in its deepest meaning, seems to have been the true character of this first temptation of Christ. And let us remember that it came to our Lord when He was least able to bear it. It is hard enough at all times to resist temptation, but to fight such a temptation as this, when the weakened bodily strength, and the pangs of hunger, gave the keenest edge to the assault of the tempter, is a task heavy enough to tax the strength of even the most resolute loyalty to God. We pitifully blame a starving man if his conscience is not over scrupulous as to the means he uses for obtaining food, and we do not realize the tremendous force with which this temptation assaulted our Lord, nor the sublime grandeur of His victory over it, if we forget that He who suffered it had been exhausted and weakened by prolonged fasting, and that it was only when the claims of the physical nature began once more to assert themselves, that the whisper of the tempter came, "Command that these stones be made bread."

But it may be asked, What would there have been sinful in Christ yielding to the suggestion of Satan, and turning the stones, by the exercise of His miraculous power, into bread? He wrought a miracle more than once to feed others, why should He not have wrought a miracle to feed Himself?

The reply to this question leads us into the very heart of the temptation, and reveals its special significance to the tempted followers of Christ in every age.

Christ was being tempted, it must be borne in mind, as man. He stands before Satan not as the Son of God — as such he was inaccessible to temptation — but as the Son of Man. He has to meet the seductions of the tempter not in His Divine power, but in the greatness of His human trust and obedience to God. He is to be "in all points tempted like as we are, yet without sin." But if our Lord had used His Divine power to satisfy His own hunger, and had wrought a miracle to supply His own pressing need, He would not have been "tempted in all points like as we are." He would have separated himself from His brethren at the very point when they would have been unable to follow Him, and in the moment of the severest Pressure of the fight would have defeated the enemy with weapons which they could never use. When the poor and needy are tortured with hunger, and the terrible temptation arises to do wrong in order to get bread, they cannot vanquish the tempter by a miracle. They must conquer, if they conquer at all, by trust; and it would be no example and no inspiration to them to be told that once their Lord and Master had been tempted as they were, but had overcome by turning the stones into bread. Christ will not overcome Satan thus. Even in the thick of the battle He will not separate Himself for a moment from the poorest and weakest of His brethren: He will vanquish His temptation, as we have to vanquish ours, not by a miracle, but by trust in the living word of God.

And hence the deep significance of the reply which Christ makes from Scripture in answer to the temptation of the devil, and with which He overcomes his assault. "It is written," our Lord says, "MAN shall not live by bread alone, but by every word that proceedeth out of the mouth of God;" and if we remember the original application of these words, and the circumstances under which they were spoken to Israel by Moses, we shall see their profound meaning as used by our Lord. Moses is reminding the children of Israel of the perils which had befallen them in the wilderness[4] — possibly this very wilderness in which Christ was now being tempted — of the way in which God had led them for forty years, "to humble them, and to prove them, to know what was in their heart, whether they would keep His commandments, or no;" and then he goes on to say, "And He humbled thee, *and suffered thee to hunger*, and fed thee with manna, which thou

---

[4] Deuteronomy 8,19

knewest not, neither did thy fathers know, that He might make thee know that man doth not live by bread only, but by every word that proceedeth out of the mouth of the Lord doth man live." Israel had been tempted in the wilderness just as Christ was now tempted; they had been "suffered to hunger," and appeared to be starving, and yet they had not perished. And why? Because God could provide and did provide "a table in the wilderness," because the last extremity of human need is only the beginning of the Divine opportunity, for when all the bread and the water had failed, the infinite resources of God were unexhausted and untouched. That was the lesson of the manna, and Christ quotes the sublime words of Moses in reference to the manna as His own reply to the temptation of the devil. He, too, is man. He, too, is in the wilderness. He, too, is tempted by hunger: tempted to distrust, and in His distrust to forsake the living God and rely on His own resources. But He refuses to yield to the temptation. God has led Him to the wilderness: God has suffered this sore need and temptation to befall Him, and God will provide a way of escape. Jesus will not work a miracle to save Himself from hunger: no! not even to assure Himself of His own Divine sonship and glory. He is here as the Son of Man, not as the Son of God; and as man, our Brother in the deepest and truest meaning of the word, He will conquer by trust in His Father's care. He lives, as well as we, not on "bread alone, but on every word which proceedeth out of the mouth of God."

And so Christ vanquishes the tempter, and we know not whether more to admire in His victory the moral grandeur of His refusal to use His supernatural power to save Himself from hunger, it may be from perishing — a refusal borne out by all His subsequent life, for never once did our Lord work any miracle for His own benefit or succor — or the gracious condescension with which He identified Himself with His brethren, by His refusal to allow Himself any support or relief in the hour of His sorest need and peril, other than that which the humblest of His disciples possess in the immeasurable resources of an unwavering trust in God.

Only once again, although in a different form, this first temptation seems to have been repeated in the life of our Lord, and repeated with

## THE FIRST TEMPTATION   55

a deadlier and darker fury, assaulting Him when even more exhausted with pain and weakness than He was in the desert. When Jesus hung on the cross, the crowd who passed by, mocked Him, and quoting His own words bade Him come down from the cross and save Himself. "Thou that destroyest the temple, and buildest it in three days, save Thyself;"[5] and the very words of the tempter in this first temptation were heard again in the jeers beneath the cross: "*If Thou art the Son of God*, come down from the cross."[6] Again, and in the hour of His deepest agony and need, He is challenged to work a miracle to save Himself from death: and again, in patient and sublime trust in God, He overcomes the temptation. The bitter taunt of the tempter, hurled at Him in the sneer, "He saved others, Himself He cannot save," while it repeats this first temptation of the wilderness, like it falls powerless before the immoveable fidelity of our Lord's trust in God.

And now let us endeavor to gather from this temptation some of the lessons it may teach us.

The temptation to turn the stones into bread so as to satisfy the hunger of the body is manifestly a type of the whole circle of temptations which arise from the needs and demands of our lower and fleshly nature. If Christ had been only apparently flesh and blood, if as many of the early heretics believed, His body was not a real body like our own, but a phantom body, which fell away from Him at His resurrection, then this temptation could never have arisen in His earthly life. It was the reality of Christ's human body which made this first temptation possible, and which gives to it all the significance it bears on similar temptations in our lives.

We, too, have bodies, and a very large part of the temptations to evil which assault us arise from the physical organization we now possess. Sometimes, indeed, temptation comes to the servants of Christ in almost literal resemblance to the form it took with their Lord, and they are hungry as He was hungry; and they are in a wilderness as He was, where there is no bread, and are tempted, as He was tempted, to break their trust in God, and in impatient unbelief to be their own

---

[5] Matthew 27:40
[6] Matthew 27:40

Providence, and to anticipate the slow movements of the Infinite Care and Love on which man alone truly lives. Sometimes the temptation arises from still lower parts of the physical nature, and the lusts of the flesh clamor for gratification, and there is a deadly strife between the animal and the spiritual, the flesh "lusting against the spirit," and "the spirit lusting against the flesh," and victory, if it be won at all, is won at such a cost that it is only less terrible than a defeat. Sometimes it is physical suffering which is the instrument the tempter uses for assailing the soul through the body. Long months, or years, of bodily agony have to be endured, making it hard to submit to the will of God, still harder to acquiesce in that will; and as the pain grows keener, and all human means of mitigation are one after another tried, and one after another fail, the terrible temptation to take life into one's own hand, and to cut it short, and by one stroke to end forever the weary days of pain, arises before the soul; or if that be thrust from us with horror, the not less deadly whisper of the tempter is heard, "Curse God and die."

In ways like these Christ's temptation repeats itself in our lives, but the chiefest peril to us of all such temptations, as it was to Christ in His first temptation, is when they take the form — and it is one of the subtlest forms temptation can take — of an inducement to satisfy lawful needs and desires by unlawful means. There was no sin in the hunger Christ suffered, and there was no sin in the desire He felt to satisfy the pangs of hunger. It was as natural and sinless a desire as the appetite with which a hungry man sits thankfully down to his food. The sin was in the temptation to satisfy an innocent bodily craving by unlawful means. For Christ to have worked a miracle to have delivered Himself from hunger would have been to have abandoned His trust in God, and would have destroyed at a blow all the blessed example His temptation and His victory in the wilderness have been to His tempted brethren in every age.

The sin was not in the desire for food, not in the longing to gratify the desire, but in the means suggested to be used for its gratification. It is so with us. Our subtlest temptations are not those which openly and bluntly seduce us to do that which is evil. Satan is far too cunning to arouse the conscience against himself at the commencement of his infernal work, for he knows full well that to exhibit temptation in all its naked and undisguised wickedness before the heart, to attempt to induce the soul to yield to sin, would be to rally to its defense whatever remained of goodness, and to make the ruin of the soul not less, but more difficult. He tempts in a subtler and deadlier way. He lays before the soul an end confessedly innocent in itself, but which can only be reached by sinful means. Then peril arises. The innocence of the end too often conceals from the conscience the guilt of the means by which it has to be attained, and the soul has fallen before temptation almost before it knew danger was near.

Thus, for example, there is no sin in the poor desiring bread; no sin in their longing to satisfy their own wants and those of their children; no sin in their desire to lessen the load of the miserable poverty under which many of them live from day to day. It is in the steps which they may take to satisfy these wants, and to lift themselves above want, that sin may lie. They may be tempted to compass a natural and rightful end by unlawful means, to imagine that since some have bread enough and to spare, while they have not enough, it cannot be wrong for those who have too little to take of the superfluity of those who have too much, so that even robbery may be justified if committed under the plea of hunger and of poverty.

So again there is no sin in a man of business desiring to make money, no sin in his ambition to attain a position which shall secure both himself and his family from pecuniary[7] care, but there may be sin of the gravest kind in the means he takes to reach the end he seeks. He may become unscrupulous in trade; he may disguise dishonesty under the plausible name of sharpness in business; he may sacrifice the peace and integrity of his conscience to getting rich, until at length an end which in itself was at least an innocent, if not a very lofty ambition, has become the means of leading him deeper and deeper into sin. Or, to take one farther illustration, and yet one to which, for obvious reasons, it is only possible remotely to allude, those dark and terrible temptations whose fires burn most fiercely in the days when youth

---

[7] Relating to or consisting of money.

is passing into manhood, and which, unless quenched, leave behind them the charred and blackened ruin of body and soul alike, derive their deadliest and most insidious peril from being, in another form, only a repetition of this first temptation of our Lord, the temptation to satisfy innocent and natural desires by unlawful and guilty means.

And now what is the one safeguard against this peril? How may we defeat this attempt of Satan to destroy the soul through the body? If we ponder the significance of our Lord's victory we shall gain the answer we seek. How, then, did Christ overcome?

Not, be it observed, by denying the legitimacy of the desires of the bodily organization. One word in our Lord's first answer to the tempter may easily escape our notice, and yet it is a word full of meaning: "Man," said Christ, "shall not live by bread ALONE, but by every word that proceedeth out of the mouth of God." In that reply the Savior expressly declares that man has a lower as well as a higher life, and He implies that this lower life demands its appropriate nourishment and satisfaction. Christ does not say, as an ascetic would have said, "Man shall not live by bread," but He says, "Man shall not live by bread *alone*;" that is, He admits and recognizes the lower needs and desires of the body, and implicitly sanctions their lawful gratification.

How then does Christ vanquish the tempter? He vanquishes him by quoting, as we have seen, a passage from the history of the children of Israel, in which Moses declared to them that their life was a nobler and diviner thing than the life of the beasts, for it was the life of "man," and man lived not on "bread alone," but on God; his truest life was not the gratification of a bodily need, but the satisfaction of the hunger of the spirit in God Himself. In other words, Christ overcame the flesh by the spirit. He conquered, not by denying either the existence of the hunger to which the temptation appealed, or His own desire for bread to satisfy it, but by asserting the supremacy for man of the higher life of faith in God. It were better for man that his body should perish from want, than that his soul should die by distrusting God.

And as Christ overcame, we must overcome too. Unhappily for the Christian life it has not not always followed the Divine wisdom of the example of Christ. It has attempted to overcome in its own way rather than in Christ's. Asceticism in every age has tried to conquer the temptations which proceed from the desires of the physical nature of man by seeking to destroy that nature altogether, instead of subordinating it to the higher laws of the spiritual life, and the result has too often been disastrous both to body and spirit. The fleshly side of man's nature is too strong for any forced and unnatural repression, and the bitterest satire on the ascetic life is the fact that it perished from sensual corruption, dragging in its fall the nobler and diviner life down to destruction as well. Only as Christ overcame shall we overcome the temptations of the flesh. We must recall ourselves to our truest and highest life; we must refuse to gratify even the most innocent desire if it necessitate our touching any means which are unholy and unlawful; we must conquer the flesh not by vainly striving to destroy the flesh, but by living above it; we must remember that the mortification of the body does not necessarily involve the mortification of the flesh; we must be willing to perish from hunger rather than abandon our trust in God. On this first temptation and this first victory of our Lord, we may read the words written which have been the secret of the spiritual life in every age, "The Just shall live by Faith."

"Then the devil taketh him into the holy city; and he set him on the pinnacle of the temple, and saith unto him, If thou art the Son of God, cast thyself down: for it is written, He shall give his angels charge concerning thee: And on their hands they shall bear thee up, Lest haply thou dash thy foot against a stone. Jesus said unto him, Again it is written, Thou shalt not tempt the Lord thy God."

Matthew 4:5–7

"And he led him to Jerusalem, and set him on the pinnacle of the temple, and said unto him, If thou art the Son of God, cast thyself down from hence: for it is written, He shall give his angels charge concerning thee, to guard thee: and, On their hands they shall bear thee up, Lest haply thou dash thy foot against a stone. And Jesus answering said unto him, It is said, Thou shalt not tempt the Lord thy God."

Luke 4:9–12

# VI
## THE SECOND TEMPTATION

In considering the instrument of the temptation of Christ we saw there was no necessity to suppose there was any literal and visible appearance of Satan to our Lord. The reality of our temptations does not depend on our seeing the tempter — nay! the force of the seductions to evil to which we are exposed often depends on the source whence they proceed, being hidden from us — and in the same way the reality of Christ's temptations in no way demands the external and bodily appearance of the tempter to Him. It is quite possible that each of these three successive temptations was, as one of them, and that the last and most terrible must have been, purely subjective to the mind of Christ; subjective, however, with this important limitation, that their origin was not subjective but objective, in other words, they did not, in the first instance, arise from within the mind of Christ, but were inducements to sin suggested by the tempter from without.

Nor is it any serious objection to this view that in the account of the second temptation we are told, "Then the devil *taketh Him* into the Holy City, and he *set Him* on the pinnacle of the temple, and saith unto Him, If thou art the Son of God, *cast thyself down*." In the vision recorded by the prophet Ezekiel (37:1) of the valley of dry bones, we read, "The hand of the Lord was upon me, *and carried me out in the Spirit* of the Lord, and set me down in the midst of the valley which was full of bones, and caused me to pass by them round about;" words which, but for the insertion of the single clause "in the Spirit," would have appeared to imply a bodily and literal translation of the prophet from the banks of the river Chebar to the desolate Mesopotamian plain where the scene of the vision is laid. There is, moreover, in the same book, a still more striking illustration of the subjective nature of the prophetic vision, and a still more striking proof that the reality of the spiritual in no way depends on its visibility to sense. A few chapters later in the same prophet (40:1), we read,

"In the five and twentieth year of our captivity, in the beginning of the year, in the tenth day of the month, in the fourteenth year after the city was smitten, in the self-same day the hand of the Lord was upon me, and brought me thither. In the vision of God brought He me into the land of Israel, *and set me upon a very high mountain*, by which was as the frame of a city on the south" — the concluding words bearing a singularly close resemblance to the terms in which our Lord's third and last temptation is described. So, too, to take one further illustration, and this time from the New Testament, we read in the Book of the Revelation (17:1–3), "There came one of the seven angels that had the seven bowls, and spake with me, saying, Come hither, I will show thee the judgment of the great harlot that sitteth upon many waters ... and he carried me away in the Spirit into a wilderness;" in which case again the translation of the seer was entirely subjective, but nevertheless real. If it be said that in the cases which have been quoted we are expressly told the translation of the prophet in the one case, and of the apostle in the other, was "in the Spirit," it may fairly be replied that this also is exactly what we are told of the temptation of Christ. "He was led up of the Spirit into the wilderness," or, as St. Luke has it, "was led in the[1] Spirit in the wilderness," the very words which, as we have just seen, are used of the translation of Ezekiel and of John.[2] There are moments of exalted experience like the rapture of which St. Paul speaks (2 Corinthians 12:2), in which he was "caught up even to the third heaven," when the share the body has in the experience is so infinitely insignificant, and so completely unnecessary to the reality of the experience itself, that it is impossible

---

[1] ἐν τῷ Πνευματί.
[2] In Ezekiel 37:1, 1, ἐν πνεύματι. — 70, In Revelation 17:3, ἐν Πνεύματι.

to say whether it was "in the body," or "apart from the body;" and so in the case of our Lord's temptation, the temptation was as real to Christ as the vision was real to Ezekiel or to John, although like the vision it was a purely subjective representation to the mind. In a dream everything seems, and for the time is, as real as our waking life, and in like manner the translation from the wilderness to Jerusalem, and the standing on "the pinnacle of the temple," with the temptation that immediately followed, were as real to Christ even if purely visionary and subjective, as if His feet had literally been placed on the summit of the pinnacle, and He had heard the voice of the tempter bidding Him cast Himself down from thence.

If this view be correct it becomes a matter of complete unimportance for us to spend any time in the attempt to determine which part of the temple is meant by "the pinnacle" to which Christ was taken by the devil. The answer to the question may have a feeble archaeological interest: it has no bearing on the significance and reality of the temptation itself.

Following the plan we have pursued in considering the first temptation, it will be well for us to study the second temptation first in its relation to our Lord; we shall then be prepared for the lessons it was intended to teach ourselves.

The diabolic subtlety of the second temptation will be seen if we consider what the first temptation and the first victory had been. That temptation, it will be remembered, was a temptation to Christ to use His Divine power on His own behalf: to satisfy His hunger and want by a miracle, and so to separate Himself from His brethren, who in their hours of need had no miraculous power on which they could fall back, and had no resource but their faith in God. Christ refused to work the miracle: refused to work it even though such a signal display of supernatural power would have quenched the awful doubt suggested by the tempter's question, "If Thou art the Son of God." He will live by faith in God. He will be "in all points tempted like as we are, yet without sin." One with us in all that belongs to our true humanity, He declares for Himself, not less than for us, "Man shall not live by bread alone, but by every word that proceedeth out of the mouth of God." Christ's first victory is the victory of a triumphant trust.

And now out of this sublime trust arises the second temptation. With equal cunning and daring, the tempter seizes the weapon with which Christ had just defeated him, and turns it against the Lord Himself.

'Thou wilt not work a miracle to supply Thyself with bread, and to save Thyself from perishing from hunger! Thou sayest Thou wilt live by trust in the care and love of God. Be it so. But dost Thou really trust, as Thou sayest? To refuse to command the stones to be made into bread because of Thy trust in God is but a small thing, for Thou art not yet ready to perish: but lo! I offer Thee a worthy test of the greatness of Thy trust. Seest Thou this dizzy height? Thou standest on the pinnacle of the temple far above the valley below: now, at length, Thou canst prove the reality and the greatness of Thy trust: Cast Thyself down: and if Thou art the Son of God, no evil shall befall Thee. Yes! If Thou art the Son of God, cast Thyself down, and Thou shalt do more than prove the greatness of Thy trust in God: Thou shalt prove the greatness of Thine own Divine Sonship as well. Thou art not yet assured of it: Thou hast given to Thyself no proof that the voice at Thy baptism, and Thine own consciousness of a Divine birth and a Divine mission, are more than a dream and a vision: Thou canst banish doubt by one supreme and triumphant act of trust in God. If Thou art the Son of God Thou wilt not, canst not perish. Nay! the very word of God which Thou hast quoted will warrant this great act of trust. Listen to it, for it is written——

> "'He shall give his angels charge concerning Thee,
> And on their hands shall they bear Thee up,
> Lest haply Thou dash Thy foot against a stone.'"

Such was the second temptation: and poorly as it has been set forth by the dark suggestions which we have thus imagined to have passed through the Savior's mind, enough has been said to show its infernal subtlety and cunning.

It appeals to the trust which had been triumphant over temptation a moment before. It does not ask Christ to separate Himself from His brethren by any miraculous exertion of His Divine power: it only bids Him commit Himself yet more fully to that care in which they and He alike have to trust. It challenges trust to nobler victories over sense and fear. Nay! it demands this new venture of faith in the interests of His Divine Sonship itself. How shall the Son of God perish with such words spoken of Him, words which declare that an angel guard shall ever surround Him, and deliver Him from so much as dashing His foot against a stone?

And now let us consider the victory of our Lord over this second temptation. We lose sight altogether of the profound significance of Christ's reply to Satan if we imagine that it was merely a quotation from Scripture forbidding Satan to tempt Him, because He was God. A far deeper meaning lies beneath Christ's words, a meaning which will become clear if we attempt to discover the original reference of the words which our Lord here solemnly uses in his answer to Satan's temptation: "Again it is written, Thou shalt not tempt the Lord Thy God."

These words are taken from the Book of Deuteronomy (6:16), but they are followed there by a significant addition which is left out by our Lord in His answer to the devil, "Thou shalt not tempt the Lord Thy God, *as ye tempted Him in Massah*." In what way did Israel tempt God at Massah? The answer is clear enough. It appears from the history in the Book of Exodus (17) that when the children of Israel in their journeyings in the wilderness came to Rephidim, "there was no water for the people to drink." They come, in bitter indignation, to Moses, and demand that he should give them water. Moses answers, "Why chide ye with me? wherefore *do ye tempt the Lord*?" One sentence, a few verses later on, lets a flood of light on the meaning of these words of Moses. After the rock has been smitten in obedience to the command of God, and a miraculous supply of water has been secured for the people, we read that Moses "called the name of the place Massah ('Temptation'), and Meribah ('Chiding'), because of the chiding of the children of Israel, *and because they tempted the*

*Lord, saying, Is the Lord among us, or not?*" Here was the sin of Israel. They refused to trust God, refused even to believe in His presence among them, unless He wrought a miracle to prove it. They came to Moses with a demand which seemed to rest on a great faith — for they asked him to supply them with water by a miracle — but which was not really faith at all, but the daring presumption of unbelief; of unbelief which refused to "wait patiently for the Lord," and openly challenged Him to prove His own presence among His people, and to justify their trust in Him, by an immediate exertion of supernatural power on their behalf.

And this was tempting God. To dictate terms of trust in God, to deny God's care and love unless He miraculously demonstrated them, to presume on the supernatural as the condition of our faith, is not faith, but unbelief; it is to dishonor God under the pretext of honoring Him. Now what was this second temptation of Christ but a repetition of the sin of Israel under a different form? The devil urges our Lord to cast Himself down from the pinnacle of the temple, in order to demonstrate to Himself the sovereign care and love of God: accepting Christ's trust which had vanquished him in the first temptation, he puts it to a new and, as it seemed, a severer and a nobler test; He is to trust God even to work a miracle to hold Him harmless in faith's most daring venture; He is to prove God to be God, and faith to be faith, by one sublime and glorious act of abandonment to the mighty power of God. But Christ refuses the temptation. He will not tempt God. Such an act as that to which Satan tempted Him would not be faith, but presumption. It might resemble faith, but only as the counterfeit coin resembles the true; and the Lord takes from the ancient history of the people of God the one illustration of unbelief daring to assume the appearance of faith, which stood in closest likeness to His own temptation, and utters for Himself, but with new and deeper emphasis, the warning Moses uttered to Israel of old, "It is written again, Thou shalt not tempt the Lord thy God."

But leaving the special occurrence in the history of the children of Israel to which our Lord refers, and returning to the temptation itself, let us endeavor to see more clearly why such an act as that of

Christ casting Himself down from the temple summit, would have been the presumption of unbelief, and therefore a guilty tempting of God, rather than the honoring Him by a great act of trust. Is there any law which can be laid down which will serve in all cases to distinguish faith from presumption; which will warn us that we are no longer honoring God by our trust, but dishonoring Him by our unbelief. There is, and it is as follows: — *The moment trust in God presumes to break any one, even the least of the laws of God, and then expects God to save it from the consequences of its disobedience, it is not trust, but unbelief, it is not faith, but presumption; it is not honoring, it is tempting God.* The laws of nature, one of which the devil was now tempting Christ to disregard and to violate, are as much God's laws as the ten commandments given from Mount Sinai; they are as truly the reflexion and the revelation of the eternal will of God as the moral law itself, and God will never require us in the interests of our trust in Him, to dishonor, by breaking, the laws which He has ordained. It was God's law that men who fling themselves down from the summit of the temple should be dashed to pieces on the ground; death was to be the wages of that sin; and for Christ first to break this law of God by casting Himself down from the pinnacle of the temple, and then to expect God to save Him from the consequences of His disobedience, was not a faith that honored God; it was a presumption which dishonored Him. And so it is with us. It is a sure and certain sign that our trust has passed from the sweetness and strength of childlike confidence in God into the impertinence of unbelief, if we find ourselves breaking the laws of God, and doing so in the expectation that God will interfere to save us from the penalties of our own transgression.

The practical applications and illustrations of this truth may be seen in almost every province of human life. When Christian parents, for instance, whose own lives are undevout and worldly, and whose homes are prayerless and unspiritual, who perhaps take a keen interest in politics, or literature, or art, or science, but manifest none whatever in the great work for which Christ died, and for which He still lives, the redemption of the world from sin, when such parents expect their children to grow up godly and devout, and to take their parents' place in the Christian Church, they are not trusting God by this expectation, they are dishonoring Him by the presumption of unbelief. They have no right, their own lives being what they are, to expect anything of the kind. They are living in daily and open violation of some of the most sacred and solemn laws of God, and there is not one word in the whole compass of Scripture to warrant them in hoping that God will interfere to save them, or their children, from the penalties of their disobedience. If they dishonor God by transgression of His laws, they must not complain if the rewards of their transgression come down on themselves, and on their children after them. To sow tares, and then expect by some Divine miracle a harvest of wheat to spring up, is to "tempt the Lord our God."

Or again: There are multitudes of Christian people who are living self-indulgent and slothful lives, but who nevertheless hope, often vaguely enough that after death, and in the day of judgment, the rewards of heaven will not be altogether denied them. They read in the New Testament of the welcome of "well done" given by the King to the good and faithful servant, and they hope such a greeting may await them; or they read of "the crown of glory which fadeth not away," and they trust that it one day may be theirs; or they catch some glimpse of the gladness and splendor of the City of God above, they hear that no tears and no darkness are there, and they trust that its splendor and bliss will be theirs when once they have entered within its golden gates. But what right have such professing Christians to expect anything of the kind? If the New Testament promises, with lavish hand, crowns and rewards in heaven, it does so under the sternest moral conditions. They are to be given to the "good and faithful servant;" to "them that overcome;" not to all that enter heaven. The Bible never conceals from us the fact that the moral inequalities we see in the Church on earth will reappear on a vaster scale in the Heaven above; that there are "first" there, and "last" there; that some servants shall have "ten cities" to rule over, but others only "five;" and that the final reward will in each case be determined by the strictest, and yet most merciful moral laws. The rewards may be, and are, of grace; but grace will never put the servant whose pound had gained ten pounds over five cities, nor put the servant whose pound had only gained five pounds over ten cities. That would be unjust grace, and paradox as the expression may sound, unjust grace — if such a thing were possible — would be a deeper offense to the moral nature than ingracious justice. What right then, we ask, have any Christians who are slothful and prayerless and self-indulgent in their lives to look for reward hereafter? Is such an expectation an act of faith, or is it not rather a great presumption? Does it not repeat, in another and widely different form, the essential sin of this temptation of Christ, inasmuch as they have first broken the known laws of the kingdom of God, and then they look to God to save them from the consequences of their disobedience. To live a Christian life which is a life of self-pleasing, to shrink from the daily self-denial which is the condition of all true discipleship of Christ, to put this world and its pleasures and rewards before the kingdom of God and its righteousness, to make the service of self the real end of life, and then to expect to be rewarded as a servant of God, is not to trust, but "to tempt the Lord our God."

Or to take one final illustration of the same sin. There are thousands of men and of women who are living altogether without God and without Christ in this world; who have never heartily and truly repented or abandoned any one sin which they really liked; who have never given to God the love He demands, nor sought from Him the mercy He is willing to bestow on all who seek it through Christ, and yet who live and who die in a vague hope that "the Almighty," as they say, will have mercy on them at the last day. Once more we ask, what right have they to any such expectation? There are laws of the kingdom of heaven as fixed and as inexorable as any of the laws of the physical universe — fixed and inexorable, because to change them in the least jot or title would be to imply that they were not originally the perfect revelation of infinite wisdom and infinite righteousness and infinite love — laws which reward obedience, and punish disobedience, as infallibly as any physical law does, and these laws are neglected, broken, trampled under foot from the beginning to the end of life, and yet it is said that at the last God will suspend their action, and mercifully and miraculously interpose to save such disobedience from its "just recompense of reward." Why? Because they trust in the mercy of God? But trust, as we have seen, which first disobeys any known law of God and then looks to Him to avert the result, is not trust; it is presumption; and to live and to die disregarding the solemn laws of the kingdom of heaven, careless of fulfilling the one supreme condition of entrance into the kingdom, and yet hoping to enter it at last, is not to trust, it is to "tempt the Lord their God."

These illustrations will suffice to show us the innumerable applications which the great lesson of this second temptation has to our daily life; there are, however, other and incidental, but not less valuable lessons which we may learn from the narrative, and which it will be well for us now to consider.

And amongst these subordinate lessons stands first this truth, that the teaching, or the apparent teaching, of any isolated text in Holy Scripture, always needs to be interpreted, and, if necessary, limited by the teaching of the whole of Scripture. There is no book in the world so precious as the Bible, and yet there is no book so easily perverted, or so perilous to those who pervert it, as this Book. It warns us itself of some who "wrest" the Scriptures "to their own destruction,"[3] and Satan's quotation of Scripture in this second temptation is an illustration of the meaning of St. Peter's words. It was a quotation, and a true quotation, from Scripture, and yet it was so quoted as to make Scripture to teach a lie instead of the truth, and to warrant Christ in an act of sin, if He had yielded to the temptation. The same perilous and illegitimate use of the Bible may be made today. It is possible to prove anything, it has been said, out of the Bible; and the statement is true, provided by "the Bible" be meant, not the whole teaching of Scripture, but the apparent teaching of isolated passages in the sacred record. It is only necessary to take a verse, to tear it out of all connection with the context, to refuse to modify its interpretation by other verses in Scripture, to quote it as if any one promise of God contained absolute and unqualified truth, irrespective of the conditions under which the promise was given by God, and you may prove that it was right for

---

[3] 2 Peter 3:16

Christ to cast Himself down from the pinnacle of the temple, as you may prove that darkness is light, or light darkness.

And even where such grievous perversions of the truth of Scripture do not take place, the same error of the misquotation rather than the quotation of Scripture may be detected in other and hardly less serious ways. There is not one heresy, there is not one form, however debased, of ecclesiastical government, there is not one eccentricity or extravagance in the Church of Christ, which has not appealed to Scripture for its justification and support. Sabellianism,[4] Swedenborgianism,[5] Spiritualism,[6] Mormonism,[7] Christadelphianism,[8] all alike quote Scripture in their defense; while the Papal Church and Plymouth brethrenism both profess to derive their distinctive ecclesiastical principles from the teaching of the Bible. The Worst systems of Church government, and the greatest errors in Christian doctrine have fled to Scripture for defense and support, and have declared they were derived from its teaching alone.

Now against this illegitimate use of Scripture Christ warns us by the use He makes of it in His answer to Satan's temptation. That solemn word "again," "It is written again," is the foundation stone on which the true use of the Bible ought to be built. Truth is unlimited, but truths are not. Each verse contains not truth, but a truth; each verse only reflecting some partial rays of the central sun of all truth. Each verse, therefore, is true, but true within limits. Take away those limits, and you destroy the truth. Just as it is the banks of a river which make it navigable, which make it indeed a river at all, so it is the

---

[4] A version of Monarchianism holding that the Godhead is a single being, differentiated only into a succession of modes or operations.

[5] The system of philosophical and religious doctrines of Emanuel Swedenborg, emphasizing the spiritual structure of the universe, the possibility of direct contact with spirits, and the divinity of Christ. This provided the basis for the New Jerusalem Church (or New Church) founded by Swedenborg's followers.

[6] The belief that because reality is to some extent immaterial it is therefore spiritual.

[7] The doctrines and polity of the Church of Jesus Christ of Latter-day Saints, founded in the U.S. in 1830 by Joseph Smith, especially its adoption of the Book of Mormon as an adjunct to the Bible.

[8] A Christian millenarian sect founded in the US about 1848, holding that only the just will enter eternal life, that the wicked will be annihilated, and that the ignorant, the unconverted, and infants will not be raised from the dead.

bounds and limits of truths which make them true; and those who would grow up into all "the truth as it is in Jesus," who would avoid all one-sided views of truth, who neither in theory, nor in practical life, would be angular or narrow, who would shun any of the intellectual or moral monstrosities professed to be founded on the teaching of the Bible, must learn first of all the many-sidedness of Holy Scripture; must read it with the light shining, not on one chapter nor on one Book, but on the whole Book; must learn how to modify and correct and supplement one Scripture by another; and must be capable of that large and wise spirit of induction which in the interpretation of Scripture, as in the interpretation of nature, always yields the richest results, building the sacred Temple of Truth, not like a mean hut of one solitary room, but like a glorious Palace, with many mansions, each with its own noble occupant, and all built according to what Scripture itself calls "the proportion of faith."

A second and not less valuable lesson taught us by the second temptation is the warning that vice is often nothing but the exaggeration and distortion of virtue. Trust in God becomes presumption, but how hard it is to say where trust ends and presumption begins. And so it is with nearly all the excellences of the Christian life. They pass by steps which are so small as to be almost imperceptible from the region of light into that of darkness. Righteous indignation against wrong degenerates into unrighteous hatred; just self-respect becomes unholy pride; healthy emulation ends in sinful envy. How easily the purest unselfishness may become conscious of itself, and feed the most subtle forms of selfishness within; what a narrow line divides the legitimate territory of the reason from those provinces where only faith has eyes to see, or feet to tread; how soon intelligent inquiry becomes presumptuous unbelief, or the submission of faith is degraded into the ignoble slavery of superstition. Our virtues might almost seem to be like the strings of a harp: stretch any one of them too far, and discord and not music is the result. Earnestness becomes severity; gentleness falls into moral weakness; activity degenerates into meddling; moderation becomes indifference; decision of character settles into dogmatic self-assertion; consideration for the feelings of others passes into moral cowardice; trust, as we have seen, goes to seed in presumption, and self-reliance in pride.

Strike any one note of human goodness and you will be sure to hear its accompanying discord. You reap the harvest, but the tares are gathered with the wheat. Goodness is not merely tainted with evil, but evil itself is too often nothing but the bastard child of goodness.

There has only been one human life in which goodness has been exhibited in its "perfect and consummate flower," every virtue making sweetest music without one discordant note, the pure light of its heavenly holiness untarnished even by the impurities which float in the sunbeams of earth — the life of the Lord Jesus Christ. We shall speak later on of the miracle of the sinlessness of Jesus — a miracle far surpassing in wonder and glory the mighty works which He wrought when on earth — but how impressive a testimony is borne by this mixed character of all human goodness, its proneness to fall away into sin, or to become exaggerated into imperfection, to the sinfulness of man. The springs of his moral life are poisoned at their fountains within. He not only does wrong, but he is wrong; and the evil with which he is born into the world taints his very efforts after goodness, so that even the tempter himself can turn the noblest achievements of holiness into occasions of stumbling, and make each successive victory over temptation a new peril to the soul.

From our achievements in the Divine life as much as from our failings comes the warning to us all, "Watch and pray lest ye enter into temptation."

"Again, the devil taketh him unto an exceeding high mountain, and sheweth him all the kingdoms of the world, and the glory of them : and he said unto him, All these things will I give thee, if thou wilt fall down and worship me. Then saith Jesus unto him, Get thee hence, Satan : for it is written, Thou shalt worship the Lord thy God, and him only shalt thou serve."

Matthew 4:8–10

"And he led him up, and shewed him all the kingdoms of the world in a moment of time. And the devil said unto him, To thee will I give all this authority, and the glory of them, for it hath been delivered unto me; and to whomsoever I will I give it. If thou therefore wilt worship before me, it shall all be thine. And Jesus answered and said unto him, It is written, thou shalt worship the Lord thy God, and him only shalt thou serve."

Luke 4:5–8

# VII
## THE THIRD TEMPTATION

We have already seen with what subtlety Satan turned the victory our Lord had gained on him in the first temptation into the instrument of his attack in the second. Christ had conquered by trust in God, and forthwith Satan bids him reveal and test the greatness of His trust by a new and more heroic venture of faith: "If thou art the Son of God, cast Thyself down: for it is written —

> "He shall give His angels charge concerning Thee;
> And on their hands they shall bear Thee up,
> Lest haply Thou dash Thy feet against a stone."

The same infernal cunning is repeated in turning the victory of the second temptation into the assault of the third. Christ had defeated Satan's challenge to His trust by refusing to admit that it was trust. To cast Himself down from the summit of the temple and to expect God to deliver Him from death was not trust, but presumption, for it was to break one of the laws of God, and then to appeal to God to save Him from the penalty of His disobedience. Such disobedience was "tempting" God.

But no sooner had our Lord vanquished this second assault of Satan than His new victory is turned into a new temptation, the last and fiercest of the three which are recorded in Scripture. Let us, with deepest reverence, endeavor to imagine the third temptation as it may have been presented to the mind of Christ, and the objective counterpart of which is found in the narrative before us. 'Not tempt the Lord thy God? Is it thus Thou speakest? But what art Thou doing now? Thou art about to begin Thy great work; to build the kingdom of God among men; to redeem a lost world from its sin and guilt, to proclaim Thyself the Prince and Savior of men. And lo! Thine own people are ready to welcome Thee as the promised Messiah, heir to the throne and the glory of David, if Thou wilt only declare Thyself their king, coming to deliver them with "a strong hand and an outstretched arm" from the hateful dominion of the Gentiles. Thou hast but to declare Thyself the Hope of Israel, and Thy work is done. The kingdom, not of Israel alone, but of the world, is at Thy feet. But Thou wilt not! Thou rejectest the crown that Thine own nation are ready to lay at Thy feet, because Thou sayest, "Thy kingdom is not of this world," and Thou art not come to be a Christ after the flesh. Can it be so? Thou needest not to abandon Thy high mission; Thou mayest use the carnal to lead to the spiritual; Thou mayest accept the earthly crown, if but for a moment; to replace it with the heavenly; Thou mayest deliver Thy people from the accursed rule of the Gentiles only to deliver them afterward from the more accursed slavery of sin. Do this, and Thy kingdom is secure. But no! Thou wilt not. Thou choosest Thine own way; Thou wilt set at naught the longings of Thy nation; Thou wilt refuse all earthly pomp and glory and power even though Thou knowest it will make Thee the "despised and rejected of men;" Thou wilt insure Thine own defeat when victory was within Thy grasp. And is not this tempting God? To cast away the only hope of success; to disappoint the multitudes who are eager and waiting for their King; to refuse the crown which they are ready to lay at Thy feet; to come to be a King and yet to disown the kingdom when it comes near to Thee; to reject the Hallelujahs the people are longing to offer Thee; to choose the lot of an outcast when the throne of a king might have been Thine; to bring down on Thyself the scorn and hatred and rejection of men, when they had offered Thee their loyalty and love; to be crucified when Thou mightest have been crowned — what is all this but tempting the Lord Thy God? Better, far better, take the crown

Thine own nation are waiting to bestow on Thee, even though it be the crown of worldly pomp and power, if by taking it "the kingdoms of the world, and the glory of them" may be Thine!'

In some such way we may imagine with all reverence the temptation to have presented itself to the mind of Christ. There have, indeed, been those who have thought that Satan literally took Christ into "an exceeding high mountain," and there literally "showed Him all the kingdoms of the world, and the glory of them," and then literally offered to give Christ "all these things" if he would "fall down and worship" him. But to say nothing of the physical difficulties and impossibilities of such an interpretation of the narrative, the spiritual difficulties which it involves are fatal to it. For Satan to have appeared as Satan to our Lord, and with bold and naked effrontery to have said to Him, "If Thou wilt worship me I will give Thee the world," would not have been tempting, but insulting Christ. Such an offer on such a condition would have been no temptation to our Lord. It would hardly be a temptation to the humblest Christian, much less to Him, to be offered a reward on condition of openly and avowedly apostatizing from God, and worshiping the devil; and we may be sure that attack with such a weapon would have made absolutely no impression on the armor of righteousness with which Christ was encompassed.

But how different all this becomes, how real, how fearfully real, the temptation is, if instead of such a mechanical and literal interpretation of the narrative, we suppose, as we are sure must more than once have been the case during the earthly life of our Lord before His crucifixion, that he was tempted by doubts as to His own Divine plan, which seemed to promise so little and to entail so much; tempted to relinquish that plan in favor of another that seemed to promise so much and entail so little. And especially would such a temptation be likely to occur at the time in Christ's life which He had now reached. He was standing, as we have seen, at the opening of His great work; nothing had yet been done, but everything had to be done; all the great and Divine purposes for which he had become incarnate had yet to be accomplished, and the kingdom of heaven, of which He was to be the King, had yet to be founded among men. It seemed to be a question, not of the end, but of the means to the end. The devil himself suggests no manner of doubt as to the end. He admits it; he offers to hasten it; he says, "All these things," that is, "the kingdoms of the world and the glory of them," "will I give Thee," provided only "Thou wilt fall down and worship me." The temptation is not to abandon the end, but to modify or to change the means which are to lead to it. And these means, as we have seen, divided themselves in the last resort into two opposite and contrasted paths: the one was Christ's, the other was the devil's.

To refuse the acclamations of the people, even though they were ready to hail Him as their King; to disappoint every hope they had formed that when Messiah came He would deliver the people of God from the hated Roman rule, and crown their race again with more than its ancient glory and honor; to change the homage of the crowd into hatred — hatred all the more bitter because of the disappointment that had led to it; deliberately to reject the earthly glory, even though it should lead to another and a nobler glory than its own; to refuse to use aught but spiritual means in founding the kingdom of God among men; to care nothing for popular applause, but very much for personal faithfulness and purity and love; to know no distinction between rich and poor, learned and unlearned, save the supreme distinction of character; to go about rebuking and denouncing wickedness even when it was found in the high places of the land; to set Pharisee and Sadducee, chief priest and ruler, in implacable hostility against Himself; to have no friend, or hardly any, save among the poorest of the poor; to associate with, and be a friend of "publicans and sinners;" to be everywhere "a sign that was spoken against;" to seem, in a word, to lose the very kingdom which He had come to establish — this was Christ's way.

And, on the other hand, to accept the glory of this world; to take the tide of national hopes and national enthusiasm at its flood; to set Himself at the head of the nation; to accept the worldly power that was ready for His use; to receive in one hour "the kingdoms of this world, and the glory of them" — this was Satan's way.

It was Satan's third temptation. It was of all temptations which could have been presented to the pure and sinless soul of Christ the most awful and searching, for it touched not Himself alone, but the great work He had come to accomplish for man. It was comparatively easy to refuse to turn the stones into bread, for His hunger concerned Himself alone; and he had learned how to endure suffering in His "Father's business;" it was not so hard, even though it involved a dread struggle, to refuse to prove His own trust in God and His own Divine Sonship by casting Himself down from the pinnacle of the temple; but to conquer this temptation, which affected not Himself, nor His own ease and comfort, but the success and glory of the work for which He had become Incarnate, was terrible indeed. And Christ knew the cost of rejecting Satan's offer. He knew that it meant disappointment, suffering, tears and blood, heartbreaking and death: He knew that it meant apparent failure of His work, the apparent loss of all He had come to save: He knew, above all, that it meant deep and deadly dishonor done to Himself as "the Son of God," and a new and tremendous guilt added to the already heavy sum of human transgression and sin. For, it will be observed, this temptation is the only one of the three temptations in which Satan suggests no doubt of the Divine Sonship and Divine glory of Christ. The doubt, "If Thou be the Son of God," is not so much as whispered here. The Divine Sonship is admitted, the full glory and dignity of Christ's person and work, of His royal honor and office, is shining on Him, and in its light the black shadow of the temptation is cast. Could a Divine Son rightly refuse the honor and glory of a Son? Could it be anything but a sin to turn His back on the only way that seemed to lead straight up to His throne? Was not this a "tempting" of God?

Such was the temptation. If we put it into its simplest and shortest form, it was the old but ever new temptation to do evil that good may come; to justify the illegitimacy of the means by the greatness of the end.

And, as such, how solemn and heart-searching are the lessons it may teach all those who profess to be servants of God among men, lessons which, perhaps, were never more needed than in the present day. We live in an age of extraordinary evangelistic zeal and effort. The type of religious life which was found in the Christian Church a hundred, or a hundred and fifty years ago, has completely changed. The edification and culture of the individual spiritual life, the "building up" of strong churches of intelligent and godly men and women, is no longer the supreme aim of Christian zeal and Christian preaching. The conversion to Christ of the unconverted, and the evangelization of the masses, absorb the energies and efforts of the Church. But the intensity of this passion for saving men may itself become a peril to the Church. In its zeal to save souls it may become indifferent to the means by which they are saved. It is altogether untrue to say, as some enthusiastic and zealous Christians are saying, that so long as men are saved it matters little or nothing how they are saved. The end, however great, never justifies unworthiness in the means by which it is attained, for in the sight of the Lord of the Church the means by which we seek to promote the coming of His kingdom are hardly less important than the kingdom itself. Nay! they are *part* of the kingdom, and to fight for victory, even for Christ, with worldly weapons, is not merely to degrade the battle of the Lord, it is to imperil the character of the victory itself. Unworthiness in the means used to extend the kingdom of God is sure to react on the kingdom itself; and converts who are won to Christ by means that are "of the earth, earthy," are too apt to retain the taint, in their spiritual life, of the soil whence they sprang. Christ might have secured apparent success; He might have enlisted the sympathies and suffrages of His own nation; He might have avoided the shame and sorrow of the cross, if He had consented to adopt worldly means to secure spiritual ends: but He would not; He rejected the temptation, and in doing so warned His disciples in every age that not even for the sake of His kingdom are they to bow down to "the prince of this world" and worship him.

But the peril of using illegitimate means for the spread of Christ's kingdom is not the only lesson taught us by this temptation; it utters another and even more serious warning to all who are followers of Christ. Satan offers Christ "all the kingdoms of the world, and the glory of them," provided only He will "fall down and worship" him. We have already seen that the inner meaning of the temptation was the attempt of Satan to induce Christ to adopt the Jewish and carnal idea of the kingdom of God prevalent in His nation, and so to seek to secure the coming of His kingdom by worldly means, but is there no profound significance in the very words used by the tempter in laying this temptation before Christ. "All these things will I give Thee, if Thou wilt fall down *and worship me*"! To resort, then, to worldly and carnal methods for the extension of Christ's kingdom; to lose faith in the power of the Gospel of Christ to do its own work, and to win its own way in the world; to seek to add to the Gospel the adventitious and meretricious "glory" of this world; to attempt, in one word, to do Christ's work with hands stained with the impurities of this world, is not to imperil merely the purity and preciousness of the work itself, it is treason to Christ and to God; it is the worship of the devil.

Would that the Church of Christ ever remembered the solemnity of this warning! The establishment of the Church by Constantine, and the secularization and demoralization of the spiritual life and energies of the Church which followed, would never have taken place if the meaning of this third temptation had been understood by the Church. The control of the Church, and the support of the Church, by the State; the association of the splendor of worldly power with the simplicity and spirituality of Christ's kingdom, may have been assented to, at first, with the simple desire to do what seemed best for the honor and glory of Christ, and for the success of His work among men; but nonetheless have its results in every age proved the fatal mistake that had been made, and warned the followers of Christ that even in His Church they may ignorantly mistake the worship of Satan for the worship of their Divine Lord and Master.

Nor is it alone in the establishment and endowment of the Christian Church by the State, and the consequent secularization of the authority of the Church, that an illustration and exemplification of this grave error may be formed. A Church may be able to boast that it has never been "in bondage to any man," that it was "born free," but nevertheless may be guilty of the sin of using worldly means for spiritual ends, and so of worshiping the god of this world. When a Church is found trusting for its success or its permanence to the wealth or social position of its members rather than to what an old mystic called "the naked arm of God;" when men are entrusted with office or power in the Church, not because of their godliness and wisdom, but because of their wealth; when the ministry so far forgets its Divine vocation, and the Divine resources open to its use, as to condescend to the lowest tricks of advertising out of the pulpit, and of sensationalism and mannerism within it, in order to attract popular notice; when the spiritual life of the members of the Church is sustained, or is attempted to be sustained, by sermons which may be full of intellectual glitter and brilliance, but are utterly destitute of the deeper and more serious elements of spiritual power, then that Church has fallen before the temptation here offered to our Lord, and is bowing down before the prince of this world and worshiping him.

And now, before considering the victory which our Lord gained over this temptation of Satan, it may be worth while to consider for a few minutes what the result would have been if Christ yielded to this temptation of the devil and had fallen down and worshiped him. There can be little doubt, we imagine, that in one sense Satan would have fulfilled his promise and have given Christ "the kingdoms of this world, and the glory of them." No cross would have stood at the end of His earthly life. There would have been louder Hosannas than Jerusalem ever offered Him as its King; there would have been vaster throngs of people proclaiming Him their Messiah and Lord; a more splendid homage from the rich and great, from rulers and Pharisees, would have been laid at His feet; in a word, Christ would have received the crown of worldly dominion and glory. But at what a cost! The great burden of human sin and guilt would have been left still resting on the world; the heart of man would have been still weary and heavy laden; the hope of immortal life would have been left a yearning and a longing, unsatisfied and unfulfilled; and the kingdom of God among men, the true and only kingdom of God in the heart, and conscience, and will of man, would have been unfounded and unknown. Christ would have lost the kingdom by appearing to gain it. The promise of the devil, like all his promises, would have turned out a black and terrible lie. He would have given the kingdoms of this world and the glory of them to our Lord, but only after Christ had given Himself to the devil. Satan would have lost nothing of his kingdom, for he would have been king of the world's king. Appearing to resign his sovereignty for a moment he would have secured it forever.

Nor is this a mere dream of unrealities and visionary absurdities. It was, at any rate, no dream to the devil. He knew the vast issues involved in the incarnation and work of Christ; knew that the Son of God had been manifested for no other purpose than to "destroy the works of the devil," and that the victory of Christ meant his own eternal shame and defeat. Twice over Satan had attempted to conquer Christ and had failed. Twice over his attack had ended in his own defeat, and now he gathers all his strength and subtlety together for one final effort; hoping that if hostility has failed to seduce Christ from His immovable loyalty to God, the offer of alliance and of friendship may succeed. "All these things will I give Thee," were his last and deadliest words to Christ, "if Thou wilt fall down and worship me."

And now let us consider the victory our Lord gained over this temptation. It is not without the deepest meaning that Christ here first addresses the tempter by his own name "Satan." "Then saith Jesus unto him, Get thee hence, Satan." It is at least possible that, up to this point, our Lord had not recognized the objective personality of the source whence the first two temptations had proceeded: they may have appeared to Him, as so many of our temptations appear to us, as mysterious suggestions rising from within the depths of His own personality; inducements to sin coming to Him, He knew not how nor whence; shadows crossing His pure mind like dark clouds floating in a clear sky. But this last temptation left no possible doubt as to the source whence these temptations had come. It revealed in lurid light the dark personality of the tempter. To do evil that good might come, or that good might apparently come; to use worldly power to secure spiritual ends; to gain the world for Himself, but to lose it for God — this was enough. Such an infernal subversion of the eternal kingdom of righteousness and truth which He had come to found, could only have proceeded from that evil spirit whose original revolt against God had cast him down "as lightning from heaven," and whose kingdom of unrighteousness and evil and suffering Christ had expressly come to overturn. Instantly our Lord answers, in words which burn with fiery indignation and scorn, "Get thee hence, Satan: for it is written, Thou shalt worship the Lord thy God, and Him only shalt thou serve."

Once again, and now for the last time, the tempter is foiled by an answer taken from the Book of Deuteronomy. "The words of all the three answers to the tempter," as Dr. Plumptre[1] well remarks, "come from two chapters of Deuteronomy, one of which (Deut. 6) supplied one of the passages (6:4–9), for the phylacteries[2] or frontlets[3] worn by devout Jews. The fact is every way suggestive. A prominence was thus given to that portion of the book, which made it an essential part of the education of every Israelite. The words which our Lord now uses had, we must believe, been familiar to Him from His childhood, and He had read their meaning rightly. With them He may have sustained the faith of others in the struggles of the Nazareth home with poverty and want. And now He finds in them a truth which belongs to His high calling as well as to His life of lowliness."

But, as in the two former cases in which Christ repelled the temptation of Satan by a quotation from the Old Testament Scriptures, there seems a special appropriateness in the answer here given to the tempter. The passage in Deuteronomy (6:13) which our Lord quotes, is followed by the significant words, "*Ye shall not go after other gods, of the gods of the people round about you.*" If we have rightly interpreted the meaning of this third temptation of our Lord as having been, in its inmost heart, a temptation to seize a present and a worldly dominion at the expense of an eternal and a spiritual kingdom, the choice of this quotation from the Book of Deuteronomy becomes profoundly significant. The one recurring peril of religion in every age is the temptation to lower its high standard of truth and of action in order to win the suffrages of the world; to seek to advance Christ's spiritual kingdom by worldly means, and what is this but a forsaking of the worship

---

[1] Ellicott, Charles John (1878). *A New Testament Commentary for English Readers*, Vol. 1 (p. 15).

[2] A small leather box containing Hebrew texts on vellum, worn by Jewish men at morning prayer as a reminder to keep the law.

[3] Another term for phylactery.

and service of the true God for the carnal idolatry of worldly success. It is the repetition of the ancient sin of Israel of old, who forsook the living God and turned to the gods of the people round about them. Christ, tempted to commit this sin, repels the temptation by quoting the very Scripture which bore the deepest analogy to the special peril in which He was now placed.

We shall see, when we come to consider the significant words with which St. Luke closes his account of the temptation, how frequently this last and subtlest temptation recurred in the life of our Lord; but before we close our study of this third temptation, let us again remind ourselves of its deepest and most solemn lesson. We may build, or attempt to build, on the one foundation, "wood, hay, stubble," but our building will never last. It will be "tried by fire," and the unworthy material which we have wrought into the eternal kingdom of truth and of righteousness will be utterly consumed in the flames. Nothing is really permanent in the spiritual kingdom but that which is spiritual. Worldly success is not true success: it is defeat calling itself a victory. Faithfulness to God may seem to delay for long ages the advent of His glorious kingdom; but it is better to wait a millennium for the coming of that kingdom than to stain its triumph, when it comes, by having fought for its King with the weapons of the god of this world. They, and only they, will be crowned at last by the King who have "contended lawfully," and even for the sake of the kingdom have refused to "bow down and worship" Satan.

"And when the devil had completed every temptation, he departed from him for a season."

Luke 4:13

# VIII
## THE LIFE OF TEMPTATION

In the preceding studies of the temptations of our Lord we have endeavored to realize the fact that they were not acts in a great drama, the issue of which had been arranged and determined beforehand, but a most real and deadly attack by the prince of this world on Him who had come "to destroy the works of the devil," and to redeem mankind from his authority and rule; an attack made on the Savior at the commencement of His redeeming work, and before that work had fully begun, in hope of overcoming the Redeemer Himself, and so of overthrowing His kingdom before its foundations had been laid among men. We have further seen that the three temptations with which the forty days of fasting and of temptation in the wilderness close, and of which alone the details are preserved in the Gospels, were essentially typical of all possible temptations of man by the evil one. They embrace in their essence the whole compass of human peril and human temptation.

The first temptation began on the lowest ground, taking for its province the sphere of the physical nature of man. The words of the tempter, "Command that these stones become bread," point to the seductions of sense, and Christ's victory over the temptation was the victory of the higher spiritual life over the fleshly appetites of the body. Whenever "the flesh" and "the spirit" meet in deadly antagonism, and these are always "contrary one to the other," we have, with whatever variation of form, a repetition in our own lives of the first temptation of our Lord.

The second temptation passed from the region of sense into the lower realm of the spiritual life, and challenged Christ's trust in God's providential care by demanding that it should prove its own reality by a transcendent venture of faith. We have seen how Christ vanquished this assault of the tempter by declaring that a trust which presumes to break even the least of the Divine laws, and then to appeal to God for salvation from the penalties of its disobedience, is not trust, but its spurious counterfeit, the presumption of unbelief.

The third and final temptation completed the cycle of possible assault. It led us into the highest region of the spiritual life, into the kingdom of Christ itself, and it warned us against the peril of using worldly means for the establishment and advancement of that kingdom, even though they promise, as they promised to Christ, a shorter road to the consummation of the kingdom, and deliverance from that cross which is the Divine way to the crown.

We see now the meaning of the words which stand at the head of this chapter, and with which St. Luke concludes his account of our Lord's temptation — "When the devil *had completed every temptation*, he departed from Him." The circle of attack had been exhausted. All possible temptation had been summed up, and had failed, in these three successive assaults made on Christ. Creation, providence, redemption had each furnished the ground of attack; the body, the soul, and the spirit had each been assailed, but in vain; the triumphant Lord had "been tempted in all points like as we are, yet without sin."

But the words which immediately follow in the narrative of St. Luke are of dark and ominous significance. "When the devil had completed every temptation, *he departed from Him for a season*." "For a season;" — what do these words mean? To what further and future conflicts do they point? Where in the life of our Lord, as recorded in the four Gospels, is the account of any renewed temptation of Christ by the devil? It is the answer to these questions that we shall attempt in the present chapter.

There is a suggestive and pregnant contrast in the words with which St. Luke closes his account of the temptations and the last words of their record in the Gospel of St. Matthew. St. Matthew closes his account thus — "Then the devil leaveth Him; and behold, angels came and ministered unto Him."[1] St. Luke, on the other hand, as we have just seen, says, "And when the devil had completed every temptation, he departed from Him for a season."

The difference in the close of the record is in profound harmony with the difference in the scope and aim of the two Gospels.[2] The Gospel of St. Matthew is preeminently the Gospel of the King, the record of the founding of the kingdom of God among men, and it closes its record of the temptation of the Christ with "the ministry of angels to a Heavenly Prince," while the Gospel of St. Luke, as the Gospel of the Son of Man, and of the suffering Savior of the world, ends its record with "a dim foreboding of the coming sufferings of the Savior." And this difference in the scope of the two Gospels will also account for the variation in the *order* of the second and third temptations in each Gospel. We have followed the order preserved in St. Matthew in the course of this exposition, but in St. Luke the second and third temptations, as recorded in the first evangelist, change places. "The preservation of the just relation of the Savior to God occupies in St. Luke the final place which St. Matthew assigns to the vindication of Messiah's independence of the world. In St. Luke the idea of a temporal empire of Christ passes more clearly into that of mere earthly dominion, which is distinctly regarded as in the power and gift of Satan. The crowning struggle of Christ is not to repress the solicitation to antedate the outward victory of His power, but to maintain His human dependence upon His Father's will. Before Messiah, the King, the temptations arise in the order of His relations to sense, to God, to man; before the *man* Christ Jesus, in his relation to sense, to man, to God."[3]

---

[1] Matthew 4:11

[2] I owe this thought to Canon Westcott's *Introduction to the Study of the Gospels*, not the least precious and suggestive of the works of one to whose writings, for the rare union they afford of the most exact scholarship with the profoundest spiritual intuition, I gladly take this opportunity of confessing my deep obligation and gratitude.

[3] Westcott, Brooke Foss (1860). *Introduction to the Study of the Gospels* (p. 295).

And now can we discover in the after narrative of the Gospels any light on the mysterious words with which St. Luke's account of the temptation ends: "When the devil had completed every temptation, he departed from Him for a season?" Four or five times, at least, in our Lord's life did specific temptation recur, and it is remarkable that on at least three of these occasions the temptation was the repetition of the last and greatest of these three temptations — the suggestion, to use Satan's own words, "to fall down and worship" him, in order to secure "the kingdoms of this world and the glory of them."

The first of these renewed assaults of the tempter of which any distinct record is preserved to us in the Gospels occurs in the Gospel of St. John, chapter 6:15. The miracle of the feeding of the five thousand had just taken place, and had made a profound impression on the multitude. For the first time Jesus had seemed to them to vindicate His claim to be "the prophet," greater than Moses, "whom the Lord God should send into the world. The miracle had recalled one of the most signal events in the history of the children of Israel in the wilderness. It was a new and more wonderful feeding of the people with food from heaven, and it was followed, we are told, by an instant revulsion of feeling in favor of the supernatural mission of Christ. "When, therefore, the people saw the sign which He did, they said, This is of a truth the prophet that cometh into the world."[4]

They resolve at once to proclaim Jesus as their Messianic King. Little did they dream of the new and terrible temptation their ignorant enthusiasm was offering to our Lord. Little did they imagine they were fulfilling the words of St. Luke, "the devil departed from Him for a season," in the earthly crown they were ready to lay at the feet of Christ. But so it was. Once more the former temptation was repeated: once more "the kingdoms of this world, and the glory of them," were offered to Christ: once more escape seemed possible from the dark and sorrowful way of the cross, and once more the possibility of the speedy advent of the kingdom dawned upon the Savior. But how did Christ meet this new temptation? The words of St. John alone are

---

[4] John 6:14

sufficient, even in their dim and mysterious suggestiveness, to hint to us both the keenness of the pain with which our Lord felt this new assault of the tempter, and the instant decisiveness with which He repelled it. "Jesus, therefore," St. John says, "perceiving that they were about to come and take Him by force to make Him a king, withdrew again into the mountain Himself alone."[5] But how immeasurably does the significance of the temptation, and of the solitary departure "into the mountain Himself alone," become heightened when we read the parallel passages in the Gospels of St. Matthew and of St. Mark. "And straightway He constrained the disciples to enter into the boat, and to go before Him unto the other side, till He should send the multitudes away. And after He had sent the multitudes away, *He went up into the mountain apart to pray*: and when the evening was come, he was there alone."[6] St. Mark repeats,[7] in other words, the same reason for Christ's departure to the mountain. The offer of the kingship to Jesus by the people was a new temptation and a new crisis in the life of Jesus, and He vanquished the peril by instant retirement and prayer.

A little later on in the life of our Lord a still more remarkable repetition of the same temptation, in which the tempter was none other than one of Christ's own disciples, is recorded in the Gospel of St. Matthew.[8] Christ had been unfolding to His disciples, for the first time with fullness and explicitness of detail, the mystery of His cross and passion, and had been showing them "how that He must go unto Jerusalem, and suffer many things of the elders and chief priests and scribes, and be killed, and the third day be raised up." To Simon Peter, not yet weaned from Jewish prejudices and Jewish hopes, the thought of a suffering and crucified King was intolerable, and with characteristic impulsiveness and vehemence he "took" Jesus and "began to rebuke Him, saying, Be it far from Thee, Lord: this shall never be unto Thee." Here was Satan's temptation over again. In the words of the disciple another than Peter had spoken to Christ. Satan had come

---

[5] John 6:15
[6] Matthew 14:22–23
[7] Mark 6:45–46
[8] Matthew 16:21–22, *seq.*

again: and once more the awful temptation, twice vanquished already, rose up before the Lord; the temptation to accept the crown which the multitude and the disciples alike were ready to lay at Christ's feet, to be a new Captain of the armies of Israel, to rally to Himself all the loyalty and patriotism of the nation; to do all this for the sake of the kingdom of God among men, and to avoid in doing it the shame and humiliation of the cross, and the execration and hatred of the very people He had come to save. All this in that single sentence of Simon Peter once more stated itself before the Lord, and the vehemence and holy indignation with which Christ instantly repelled the dark suggestion bore tragic witness to the pain and the peril which this renewal of temptation caused the Lord. "He turned," we read, "and said unto Peter" — almost repeating the very words He had spoken to Satan at His third temptation — "Get thee behind Me, Satan: thou art a stumbling block unto Me: for thou mindest not the things of God, but the things of men." And then follow the words, so solemn and piercing, which told the disciples, as they tell Christ's disciples in every age, that the only way to the kingdom of God on earth is the way of the cross: "Whosoever would save his life shall lose it: whosoever would lose his life shall find it."

The third recurrence of this temptation took place nearly at the close of Christ's earthly life, and just before the anguish in Gethsemane.

Every detail in the narrative is full of meaning.

The first dim signs of the coming conflict begin on the day of the triumphal entrance into Jerusalem, when the air was rent with the Hosannas of the multitude crying, "Blessed is He that cometh in the name of the Lord: Blessed is the kingdom that cometh, the kingdom of our father David: Hosanna in the highest."[9] Once more the earthly crown seemed within our Lord's grasp, and "the kingdoms of this world, and the glory of them," spread themselves before His view, so that even the Pharisees "said among themselves, Behold, how ye prevail nothing: lo, *the world is gone after Him*."[10] Again, temptation was near. The conflict, however, did not fully begin until the day but

---

[9] Mark 11:9–10
[10] John 12:19, *seq.*

one after this triumphal entry. "Certain Greeks" had desired, we are told, to "see Jesus." In them Christ sees the first fruits of His redeeming work among the Gentiles. "The hour is come," Jesus says, "that the Son of Man should be glorified." But the mention of His own glorification at once suggests the dark and sorrowful way through which alone His glory could be reached, and He adds, with that peculiar and marked solemnity and impressiveness which were always indicated by the prefixed "Verily, verily," "Verily, verily, I say unto you, except a grain of wheat fall into the earth and die, it abideth by itself alone; but if it die, it beareth much fruit." And then significantly follow the same deep and solemn words which, as noted, closed the account of Simon Peter's temptation of Christ, "He that loveth His life loseth it; and he that hateth his life in this world, shall keep it unto life eternal." Immediately after these words the conflict once more begins. "Now," exclaims the Lord, "is My soul troubled; and what shall I say." For one moment, and only for one moment, as the dreadful shadow of the cross cast itself over His path, and as the awful anguish of Gethsemane and of Calvary began almost to be tasted by Him who came "to bear the sins of the world," there was a human shrinking from the cup which His Father had given Him to drink. Could it be that there was no other way to the Crown but through the Cross? "Father," Jesus cried, "save Me from this hour." The next words check the natural shrinking from the Cross — "But for this cause came I unto this hour." And the answer quickly came. Only in the greatest moments and crises of Christ's life on earth, do we read of heaven being opened, and of the voice of God speaking to His Eternal Son; but such a moment and such a crisis were now pressing on the soul of Jesus, and instantly "there came a voice out of heaven, saying, I have both glorified it, and will glorify it again."

The victory was once more won; and with new and triumphant joy Jesus cries, "Now is the judgment of this world: NOW SHALL THE PRINCE OF THIS WORLD BE CAST OUT, AND I —" for the division of the words of Jesus into verses hide from us the close connection of the Cross of Christ with the casting out of Satan. "IF I BE LIFTED UP FROM THE EARTH, WILL DRAW ALL MEN UNTO ME."

He who had told His disciples of those who gained their life by seeming to lose it, would Himself gain the world by seeming to lose it. His Crown was His Cross, and His Cross was His Crown.

One final crisis in the life of Jesus is recorded in the Gospels. Hitherto each successive assault of the tempter had been triumphantly beaten back, and now the time of conflict was drawing to a close. There remained but one more opportunity to the prince of this world of tempting its Prince and Savior before His death on the Cross, with which the victory would be finally won. Gethsemane still intervened between the struggle in the upper room and the crucifixion, and it is in Gethsemane the last conflict takes place. It is true, indeed, that the Gospels make no express mention of any temptation by the devil in the Garden of Gethsemane, but the same thing may be said of the three previous occasions which we have just been considering, and on which, as we have seen, there is no reason to doubt temptation was offered to Jesus. We shall find, moreover, that there are words spoken by Christ during this awful struggle in Gethsemane which seem to imply that to His mind there were present more than the bitter shame and anguish of the Cross, more even than the intolerable agony of bearing away the sin of the world; there was also present the dark and malignant work of one who, even in that awful hour, had not abandoned the hope of overcoming the Captain of our salvation.

The narrative begins with words which plainly recognize the presence of the tempter in the betrayer. "And Satan entered into Judas," we read,[11] "who was called Iscariot, being of the number of the twelve." The final assault of the devil is to be made once more through one of the disciples of the Lord. Judas is to repeat, in another form, the sin of Peter. Shortly after, the Passover feast begins, and hardly has it begun when for the first time in His intercourse with His disciples Christ makes open reference to the temptations He had endured. "Ye are they which have continued with Me in My temptations;"[12] and then He adds, connecting the coming kingdom in some mysterious way with His own endurance of, and triumph over temptation — "And I

---

[11] Luke 22:3
[12] Luke 22:28

appoint unto you a kingdom, even as my Father appointed unto Me, that ye may eat and drink at My table in My kingdom; and ye shall sit on thrones judging the twelve tribes of Israel."[13] But with the thought of His own temptations and conflicts with the devil still uppermost in His mind, He turns to Peter, and warns him of the conflicts through which he will have to pass before he enters the kingdom. "Simon, Simon," Christ says, "behold, Satan asked to have you, that he might sift you as wheat: but I made supplication for thee, that thy faith fail not: and do thou, when once thou hast turned again, stablish thy brethren."[14] The Passover meal is eaten; the disciples' feet are washed by the Lord, thus silently rebuking their "contention" which of them was "accounted to be greatest;" the reference to the betrayer, who was still present with the twelve, grew more and more pointed, until at length, as if unable longer to endure his presence, and as if longing to terminate the dreadful suspense, Jesus openly turns to Judas and says, "That thou doest, do quickly." The institution of the Lord's Supper, the Passover of the Christian Church, follows, when once again the dark shadow of the tempter crosses the path of Jesus. "The prince of the world," Jesus says, "cometh; and" — sure of victory even before the last conflict begins, He adds — "He hath nothing in Me."[15]

Gethsemane followed. No heart but the heart of Jesus Himself can ever measure the depth of its unutterable anguish and woe; none but those to whom God has revealed the meaning of that single word "sin" can so much as faintly understand the tremendous burden of human guilt which then began to rest on the sinless sin-bearer: but we may catch some distant vision of His woe if with unsandaled feet we follow our Lord over the holy ground.

Only once before during His life had Jesus ever spoken of His personal suffering, but now He cannot be silent. The pressure is too great, the anguish too awful to be self-contained. He begins, in the impressive language of St. Mark, to be "greatly amazed, and sore troubled."[16]

[13] Luke 22:29–30
[14] Luke 22:31–32
[15] John 14:30
[16] Mark 14:33

And then He turns to the three disciples whom He had taken with Him that they might "watch" with Him — as if in the dread conflict on which He was now entering He longed for the succor of their vigilance as well as of His own — and utters the pathetic words, "My soul is exceeding sorrowful even unto death."[17] Then He withdraws Himself a little way — "about a stone's cast" — from them, and there alone with His Father pours out His soul in that sublime but awful prayer, every word of which quivers with agony, "Abba, Father, all things are possible unto Thee: remove this cup from Me: howbeit not what I will, but what Thou wilt."[18]

He returns to His disciples and finds them "sleeping," — St. Luke adds, "for sorrow," — and once more He warns Simon Peter of the perils of those temptations of the devil of which Peter knew as yet so little, and Christ knew so much. "Simon, sleepest thou? Couldest thou not watch one hour? Watch and pray *that ye enter not into temptation*."[19] A second time Jesus leaves the disciples and prays the same prayer. A second time He returns to them and finds them sleeping. A third time He leaves them — this constant change of place being the reflection of the agitation and conflict which were going on within — and a third time He prays the same prayer, but now with such augmented intensity of anguish that "His sweat became as it were great drops of blood falling down upon the ground."[20] A third and last time He returns to the disciples, and once more repeats the solemn warning, "Why sleep ye? Rise and pray *that ye enter not into temptation*."[21]

It is as these words are being uttered that Judas with his band draws near. The last damning act of human ingratitude and sin is consummated in the traitor's kiss, but as Jesus is "betrayed into the hands of men," the last words He utters in the Garden of Gethsemane disclose the presence of a vaster hostility than even the hatred of "the son of

---

[17] Mark 14:34
[18] Mark 14:36
[19] Mark 14:38
[20] Luke 22:44
[21] Luke 22:46

perdition:" "This is your hour," the Lord says, "AND THE POWER OF DARKNESS."[22] His own words were fulfilled, "The prince of this world cometh and hath nothing in Me."

We shall consider later on the significance of that ministry of angels which followed the final victory over Satan in the wilderness, but it may be noticed here that it is not without the deepest meaning that in Gethsemane, and in Gethsemane alone, does this angelic ministry reappear in the life of Christ. The last great temptation is accompanied, as the first was, by supernatural succor, and the evangelist who closed his account of the temptation in the wilderness with the words, "The devil leaveth Him for a season," and who records the return of the tempter in the conflict in Gethsemane, with "the power of darkness," records also at the close of the struggle the heavenly refreshment which was sent to our Lord; — "there appeared unto Him an angel from Heaven strengthening Him."

We have already referred to the possible recurrence during the crucifixion of another of these three wilderness temptations of our Lord. It is, at least, remarkable that the very words Satan here uses, challenging Christ to prove His Divine Sonship by a miracle, are again heard in the scornful mockery of the crowd beneath the Cross, "If Thou art the Son of God, come down from the Cross:"[23] and it can hardly be doubtful that He who was "made in all points like unto His brethren;" who was in very deed our Brother; who was conscious as we are of the natural shrinking of the body from pain; whose death, above all, as the Divine Sacrifice for the sins of the world, overwhelmed Him with a woe of which we can know but little, must have felt the natural and sinless longing to end in a moment, by His own Divine power, the torment of the Cross, and to declare by one last transcendent miracle that He who was crucified in weakness was in very deed the Son of God. But Christ's triumph in the wilderness over Satan was only augmented in the voluntary obedience of the eternal Son "to death, even the death of the cross." He had come "to save others," and Himself He would not save.

---

[22] Luke 22:53
[23] Matthew 27:40

The last act of Christ's human life — if we may dare to speak of degrees of glory in that one all glorious life — was the sublimest moment in His moral life. "Tempted in all points like as we are," He is tempted even in death; but sinless in death, as He had been sinless in life, He dies triumphant over sin, and in the hour of His apparent defeat wins His last and greatest victory over the empire of darkness and of Satan.

We have thus examined the principal crises in the life of our Lord which the Gospels record, and as we have seen the recurrence in each of them of special temptation. They lose, indeed, a great part of their significance if the infernal hostility of Satan to Christ which prompted the first temptation, and which reappeared in these subsequent assaults, be overlooked or forgotten. The wilderness did not and could not exhaust the "wiles of the devil." His antagonism to Him who had come to "destroy the works of the devil" did not cease with his defeat at the beginning of Christ's ministry. His hope of vanquishing "the Captain of our salvation" was not destroyed by the failure of his first great attack on the kingdom of God which Christ had come to establish among men. One defeat does not lead the devil to abandon his assaults on us; nor did our Lord's first defeat of the tempter end his temptation of Him. The life of Christ was a life of temptation, for it "behooved Him in all things to be made like unto His brethren."

But if this were so, it is impossible to believe that the instances of temptation which we have been considering were all the temptations which Christ endured subsequently to His temptation in the wilderness. His life, from first to last, was a tempted life, and as no day passes in our own experience in which we do not find some seduction to sin beset our path, so we may believe that He too found "occasions of stumbling" at every step in His earthly life. Those "spiritual hosts of wickedness in the heavenly places" which never cease their warfare against the soul of man, did not, we may be assured, leave "the Son of Man" alone. Nay! they would be less likely to leave Him alone than to leave us alone, for victory over any one of us would only mean one more private soldier in the great army of the Lord fallen in the field, but victory over Christ — if even in imagination we may conceive for a moment the inconceivable — would have been the vanquishing of the "Leader and Commander of the people," the destruction of the kingdom of God by the conquest of its King.

Was there no temptation to our Lord — to take only a few illustrations from the life of Christ — in the poverty of His earthly life? Do not the poor, the "dim and common populations" of our great cities, know too well that if poverty shuts some of the gateways by which sin finds access to the soul, it opens many which are closed to the rich. And can we doubt for a moment that He who "for our sakes became poor," who "had not where to lay His head," who lived all through His public life on the charity of those who "ministered to Him of their substance," chose that lot, not only because it was the lot of the vast majority of His brethren on earth, but because it enabled Him to encounter the same spiritual perils which beset the poor in every age? And they who are called to follow their Lord in the poverty of their earthly life, and are tempted to "curse God and die" because of the hardness of their lot, may remember Him who is "not ashamed to call them brethren," who lived a poor man's life with unrepining submission to the will of His Father, and who is the One perfect example to "them that are poor in this world" of being "rich in faith and heirs of the kingdom which God hath promised to them that love Him."[24]

Was there no temptation to our Lord in the hopeless indifference and deadness of the people, in the bigotry and blindness of those who were "teachers in Israel," above all in the dullness and "slowness of heart to believe" of His own disciples? Do not those who with unworthy steps strive to follow Christ know how hard it is to be "kind to the unthankful and to the evil," and how easy it is to lose heart in work for God, worn out by the stolid indifference and ignorance and ingratitude of those whom they are seeking to lead to God? And this temptation does not diminish, but increases with the earnestness of our zeal for God and for the salvation of men. The follies and perverseness of the multitude most keenly affect those who

---

[24] James 2:5

are seeking to bless them, for the selfish and self-absorbed can know nothing of the temptation to lose faith in man, and all hope of his redemption, which is the daily experience of all who are seeking "to save the lost." But if we whose hearts are tainted with selfishness feel this, how much more keenly must He have felt the pressure of this temptation who never knew one selfish desire, who came "not to be ministered unto but to minister," who "pleased not Himself"? And yet He never yields to it. He is the same patient, gentle Teacher to the froward and ignorant, that He is to the simple and guileless. Not one hasty word, not one petulant expression, ever escapes His lips. He speaks, it is true, burning words of rebuke and anger against hypocrisy and self-righteousness and malignity of heart, but in the midst of the most terrible indignation with those who were "blind leaders of the blind," His love and forbearance are as unruffled by the ingratitude and obstinacy and sin of men as the depths of the ocean by the storms which lash its surface into fury and wrath.

Was there no temptation to our Lord, to take only one farther illustration from the Gospels, in the activities of His public life — activities so incessant that we read there was not, at one time, "leisure so much as to eat" — to lose the intimacy and freshness of His communion with the Eternal and Unseen? We know, alas! how often a life of active and exhausting service for God in the world is unfriendly to devoutness of spirit: how quickly may we lose the spirit of prayer in the excitement and strain of spiritual work; how hard it is to be in the world and yet not of it, and how easily we excuse ourselves in remissness of prayer, or neglect of our own spiritual culture, by the plea of fatigue incurred in the work of God. But it was never so with Jesus Christ. Engaged, and ceaselessly engaged, in laboring for others, in "preaching the Gospel of the kingdom," in going about "doing good," He never loses the sacredness and nearness of His Father's presence; at the end of the heaviest day of labor recorded in the Gospels, He rose up, we read, "in the morning a great while before day, and departed into a desert place, and there prayed."[25] His feet trod the roughest

---

[25] Mark 1:35. Compare the parallel passages.

ways of our earthly life, but His face was ever turned up to heaven and touched with the light of God. He shared with us every experience of human weakness and weariness, but never once did He allow the pressure of the most absorbing work to interfere with His God. He was among us as "one that serveth," and yet, to use His own sublime words of Himself, He was ever "the Son of Man who is in heaven."

The life of temptation was also a life of uninterrupted victory over temptation. "He was tempted in all points like as we are, yet without sin."

And it is in this light that the sinlessness of Jesus becomes so amazing. It has been asserted by a skeptical criticism that the miracles which the Lord Jesus is declared in the Gospels to have wrought are inconsistent with the "laws of nature," and are therefore unbelievable by "the modern scientific intellect," but that if the Christian Church would be content to accept the lofty ethical teaching of Jesus of Nazareth, *minus* the miracles, no great difficulty in the way of faith would remain to the reason. No mistake can be greater. The miracles wrought by Christ are not the only, or the most startling miracles of the Gospel. Christ Himself is His own greatest miracle. His absolute sinlessness, His freedom from the least taint of human infirmity and folly, His pure and perfect life, are a far more wonderful exception to the so-called "laws of nature" than the healing of the sick, or the stilling of the storm, or the raising of the dead. For not only was Jesus "without sin" in the outward acts of His life, but He was free from that consciousness of a sinful nature, of an inherited bias toward evil, which makes its appearance with the first dawn of consciousness in every other human life; and it is only when we remember that this sense of sinfulness is as truly a "law of nature" as any of the great laws of the physical universe that, to use the words of the late Professor Mozley — perhaps the profoundest thinker of the English Church since the time of Bishop Butler — "the sinlessness of Christ appears in its true light as a supernatural fact — an inward invisible miracle surpassing in wonder any of the visible miracles which He wrought."[26]

---

[26]  Mozley, James Bowling (1883). *Lectures and other Theological Papers* (p. 147).

It is idle to imagine that it is possible to get rid of the supernatural in the Gospels by blotting out the miracles wrought by Jesus. The miracle *of* Jesus remains; the miracle of a human life, in all other respects like our own, save in this, that it was "without sin;" the miracle of a will ceaselessly assaulted by every temptation "common to man," but as ceaselessly victorious over each successive assault; the miracle of a character, from the first hour of life to the last, unconscious of evil; the miracle of a goodness touching, like the sunlight, the darkest and most festering pollutions of this world, and remaining as untainted as the sunlight by contact with impurity; and so long as this supreme manifestation of the supernatural meets us on every page of the Gospel history, it is worse than a waste of time to be discussing the possibility of the miraculous. Here it is, breathing, living, moving before our eyes, an Image too fair for the heart of man to have conceived if it had not seen its heavenly beauty in the flesh, and an Image the spell of which for eighteen centuries has enchained the wonder of foes as well as of friends, so that even unbelief has been compelled to exclaim, "If the life of Socrates was the life of a saint, the life of Jesus was the life of God."

"Then the devil leaveth him, and behold, angels came and ministered unto him."

Matthew 4:11

# IX

## THE MINISTRY OF ANGELS

"Behold, angels came and ministered unto Him."

Such is the close, according to St. Matthew's Gospel, of the great temptation of our Lord. We have already seen the significant contrast this ending to the temptation affords to its close in the Gospel of St. Luke, and it now remains for us to study the significance of this angelic ministry as recorded in "the Gospel of the King."

It is true that Scripture tells us less of the ministry of angels in the New Testament than it does in the Old. The messengers and heralds of the King pass out of sight when the King Himself appears, but there is one verse in the first Epistle of Peter which seems for a moment to lift the veil which hides the heavenly intelligences from us, and shows us them following with the deepest interest the footsteps of their Lord and King on earth. After speaking of "the salvation" concerning which "the prophets sought and searched diligently, who prophesied of the grace that should come unto you; searching what time or what manner of time the Spirit of Christ which was in them did point unto, when it testified beforehand the sufferings of Christ, and the glories that should follow them," the apostle adds that there were other intelligences than the prophets, who longed to know the mystery of a crucified and glorified Savior, "which things," St. Peter says, "angels desire to look into."[1] And the word the apostle uses[2]

---

[1] 1 Peter 1:10
[2] παρακύψαι.

implies far more than the English expression "to look into" conveys to our ears. It is the "earnest gaze of one who bends over a given object and scrutinizes it thoroughly,"[3] which is implied in the apostle's word, and it gives us, though for a moment only, a revelation of the eager and reverent interest taken by these high intelligences of heaven in all the facts of the life of their King when on earth.

We do not wonder, then, to find that when Christ appears on earth, these spirits who had never sinned, who had bowed in adoration in heaven before His glory, who had long desired to know the meaning of the strange predictions of inspired men concerning Him, should have appeared too. "An angel of the Lord" appears to Zacharias to announce the birth of John the Baptist, the Lord's forerunner.[4] The angel Gabriel announces to the Virgin Mary the coming birth of her Savior and her King.[5] The heavens are filled with "a multitude of the heavenly host" praising God at the birth of Jesus.[6] "An angel of the Lord" warns Joseph to depart into Egypt,[7] and "an angel of the Lord" bids him return again to the land of Israel.[8] At the Passion in Gethsemane "there appeared an angel from heaven strengthening Jesus."[9] At the Resurrection the stone is found removed from the mouth of the sepulcher, "an angel of the Lord" having "descended from heaven and rolled away the stone."[10] Mary sees "two angels in white sitting one at the head, and one at the feet, where the body of Jesus had lain."[11] And as each of the great events of our Lord's earthly life has been thus attended by the ministry of angels, so at the Ascension of Jesus they wait to follow their King to the everlasting glory, and announce to His

[3] Plumptre *in loc.* in the Cambridge Bible for Schools.
[4] Luke 1:11
[5] Luke 1:26
[6] Luke 2:14
[7] Matthew 2:13
[8] Matthew 2:19
[9] Luke 22:44
[10] Matthew 28:2
[11] John 20:12

disciples as they were "looking steadfastly into heaven" the return of their Lord in the power and majesty of the Second Advent.[12]

There was nothing, therefore, exceptional in this ministry and succor of the angels being offered to our Lord at the close of the temptation. It was only a part of that service which they rendered the Savior throughout His earthly life — service which was the crowning joy of the angelic host. For the Lord Jesus Christ had come from heaven. He had been the light and glory of the city of God above. For ages upon ages, long before man was created, He had received the adoration and worship of countless myriads of angels who stood before His throne. The mighty cherubim, "eldest born of the intellectual creation of God," had gazed in fixed and unbroken wonder and awe at the "treasures of wisdom and of knowledge" which were hidden in Him who was the Eternal Word, the uncreated "Reason" of the Most High. The burning seraphim, spirits of worship and of love, had fed their rapt devotion from the fount of living fire ever glowing in the infinite heart of Jesus; and angels and archangels, filled with the awful vision of His glory, and standing in the light streaming from His throne, had fallen prostrate before Him as they heard the Divine command, "Let all the angels of God worship Him." Their ministry on earth was only a continuation of the sublimer ministry of heaven.

Nor has their ministry ceased with the Ascension of our Lord. If our conflicts with temptation, and our victories over the devil are like those of Christ in their severity and peril, they are like them also in their end and crown. The glorified Lord does not deny to His tempted followers the succor and help which He found so precious in His hour of earthly need. "Are they not all ministering spirits," says the author of the Epistle to the Hebrews, "sent forth to do service for the sake of them that shall inherit salvation?"[13] They whose harps are struck to a louder strain of joy over "one sinner that repenteth," do not watch with indifference the long struggles which precede and follow true repentance for sin. They wait with eager interest the issue of our

[12]  Acts 1:10
[13]  Hebrews 1:14

conflicts with evil, and they come to visit us with their gracious ministries when the struggle is over, as they came to Jesus.

How they come, what they do for us when they come, we may not be able to tell; but we may owe more than we know to the willing, if unknown service they render in our hour of need. He who is their Lord and ours may give them some special mission of help and of love for us when we most need it; and many a time the healing of the wounds inflicted in the strife, the quieting of the storm which had been raging within, the whispering of new hope and new courage to the depressed, the warding off of unsuspected attacks of the innumerable hosts of darkness when we were too weak to meet them, may be owed to the silent and blessed ministry they render to us.

> "Whenever, in some bitter grief, we find
> All unawares, a deep, mysterious sense
> Of hidden comfort come, we know not whence;
> When suddenly we see, where we were blind;
> Where we had struggled, are content, resigned;
> Are strong where we were weak,
> And no more strive nor seek;
>
> "Then we may know that from the far glad skies
> To note our need, the watchful God has bent,
> And for our instant help has called and sent,
> Of all our loving angels, the most wise
> And tender one, to point to us where lies
> The path that will be best,
> The path of peace and rest."

But the ministry of angels to our Lord is more than a witness to His royal majesty, it also attests the reality and severity of the struggle with the devil through which the man Christ Jesus had passed.

Even if the final assault of the tempter had not been preceded by the long and exhausting fast of forty days, if there had been no other demand on the energies, both physical and spiritual, of the Lord Jesus than that involved in the struggle which was now for a season over, we can imagine the terrible reaction and exhaustion which must have followed such a contest. If the soldier is wearied and faint on the evening of the day of the battle, when its fierce excitement is gone, and the tumult of the conflict has ceased, how much more must such a spiritual conflict as that through which "the Captain of our salvation" had been passing, have ended in utter prostration and weakness. We know from our own experience a little of the sense of physical feebleness which ensues when any great spiritual crisis in our history has been passed, or when the forces of good and of evil have been arrayed on the battleground of our own soul, and we have had to fight for victory over some deadly sins, but we cannot tell how much a conflict on which was hanging the destiny of a world must have involved for the Lord Jesus Christ. And when to the tremendous issues of the struggle we add the fact that it took place at the end of a prolonged and exhausting fast, we may perhaps faintly imagine how utterly the Victor must have been "spent" at its close, and how welcome the boon this ministry of angels must have been to Him who, because "the children were sharers in flesh and blood, also Himself in like manner partook of the same."

But if the angelic succor granted to our Lord attests the greatness of the spiritual conflict through which He had gone, it is an incidental but most precious proof to us of the completeness with which He had identified His lot with that of His brethren. He will work no miracle to supply His own hunger at the commencement of His temptation. He will not, now all is over. He will do nothing that shall in any way separate Him from His tempted brethren in every age. He began the conflict as man. He ends it as He began. Conscious of power that in a moment could have turned the stones into bread, and made weariness vanish before Almighty strength, He will not use His power. He submits to be ministered unto, and the Creator of all worlds is succored by the creatures whom He had made. In the hour of His triumph we may read a new meaning in the gracious words, "We have not a High Priest that cannot be touched with the feeling of our infirmities; but

One that hath been in all points tempted like as we are, yet without sin."[14]

Nor is the reality of the humanity of our blessed Lord, as witnessed by His temptation and by the ministry of angels which followed it, a doctrine of purely theological interest and without relation to our spiritual life.

The worship of the Virgin, and the place assigned to her, in the devotions of the Roman Church would never have been possible if that Church had not first lost the vivid and tender realization of the true humanity of Jesus which pervades the New Testament, and was the life and joy of the faith of the early Church. Christ was farther and farther withdrawn from all real and true participation in the lot of men, and while the theological doctrine of His humanity remained untouched, the living sense of that humanity became fainter and fainter, until at length the way to God which He had opened through the veil of His flesh was lost, and His mother was invoked to occupy the place which He alone can ever fill. It may be true that the denial of the Deity of Christ has even graver results for the spiritual life of the Church than the forgetfulness of His humanity, but it is equally true that without the humanity, the Deity of our Lord is removed from all practical relation to the religious life of mankind. We cannot afford to lose any part of "the truth as it is in Jesus:" the Deity of Christ, not less than the Humanity, and Humanity not less than the Deity, or rather as we prefer to say, the unique personality of Him who was not merely God *and* Man but the God-Man, is as essential to the vigor and health of the spiritual life as it is to the soundness and accuracy of its creed. Romanism[15] warns us of the peril that follows those who deny the one; Unitarianism[16] warns us in equally impressive tones of the peril of denying the other.

But the realization of the true humanity of Jesus in His temptation, as witnessed by the ministry of angels, is necessary not only to bring

---

[14] Hebrews 4:15
[15] Roman Catholicism.
[16] A person, especially a Christian, who asserts the unity of God and rejects the doctrine of the Trinity.

His temptations near to our own, and to enable us to realize the depth of His sympathy with us, it is also necessary to the reality and vividness of our sympathy with Christ in His struggle with the tempter. We have already briefly referred to the danger there is of the Church losing the tenderness and warmth of the love which the first disciples had to Christ, and of our forgetting the sympathy we ought to offer our Lord in the sympathy we are so eager to expect from Him. We can hardly wonder if our love for Christ grows less intense and warm, and the fountains of feeling in the heart of the Church are dried up, if the temptation be conceived as a dramatic conflict, the result of which had been determined upon and arranged beforehand. The moment we feel it was a real struggle, involving exhaustion, pain, and peril to Christ Himself; taxing His human energies to their very uttermost by the grievous strain; prostrating Him at its close in such weakness, that "the angels came and ministered unto Him," the heart leaps up in joy and gratitude to its Savior and King, and knows not whether most to wonder at the love which for our sakes willingly endured so fierce a conflict, or the glorious goodness which quenched in successive triumphs "all the fiery darts of the devil."

And we are tempted too. But temptation becomes a new thing to the soul if it realizes that in the struggle with the tempter, in the weariness and weakness of the conflict, in the moments when defeat seems inevitable, nay! in those victories which are only less terrible than a defeat, Christ is with us all through. We are sure, at least, of His sympathy, whosoever else may fail us; sure of His most tender and generous pity; of His making allowances, which none but Himself could make; sure even in the hour of defeat — for defeat as well as victory comes, alas to us all — that He will not judge us too harshly, for He knows, as none of us can ever know, "the depths of Satan," and on the throne of the eternal glory He "remembereth our frame; He knoweth we are but dust."

But we may learn another lesson of not less practical importance from the heavenly ministry granted to the Lord at the close of His temptation. Christ had been tempted falsely to rely on the ancient promise of God to His people, "He shall give His angels charge over

Thee," and to cast Himself down from the summit of the temple, and He had refused to tempt God, even though He lost the succor which in such an hour of need the angels could render to Him. He missed, as we should have said, the celestial ministry ever ready to be granted to the children of God, and above all, to Him who was the Son of God. He refused to avail Himself of the angelic "charge" because He refused to "tempt God."

But the ministry which appeared to have been lost in the temptation is found at its close, in the succor of the ministering angels, and found not then alone, but in even richer abundance earlier in the life of our Lord, for only a few days after the temptation we find Christ saying to Nathanael, "Verily, verily, I say unto you, Ye shall see the Heaven opened, and the angels of God ascending and descending upon the Son Man."[17]

And so we may learn for ourselves the homely, but ever needed lesson that the self-denials of the path of duty are never real losses to the soul. No doubt this truth may be so represented, or misrepresented, as to be turned into a falsehood to the conscience and a dishonor to God. It may be said that it comes simply to this, that goodness *pays*, and that therefore the service of God and of righteousness becomes in the end a question of policy and of self-interest. But this is a caricature, not a statement, of the truth. If I resist temptation to do wrong *because*, and only because of the reward promised to them who overcome, I am not morally the victor over sin. I am really yielding to one temptation while professing to resist another. I am putting self and not God first, and no man is a servant of God who has not learned that the essence of all goodness lies in putting God before self, and that to make obedience to the will of God the result of a calculation of the advantages of obedience, is to dethrone the will he professes to obey.

But, on the other hand, it is true — and generation after generation of men and of women who have "suffered for righteousness' sake" have proved its truth — that wherever and whenever right is done, not

---

[17] John 1:51

from policy but from principle; where temptation to sin is vanquished, not because it will pay in the long run to resist, but because of the inner loyalty of the soul to God; where self-denial has been freely and gladly borne without a thought of the reward, and only because sacrifice is the sweet necessity of love, God will more than compensate the soul, even in this life, for the loss; and the blessings which seemed to have been lost, because we loved Him better than we loved ourselves, come back multiplied and augmented a thousandfold to the heart.

Abraham surrenders "his son, his only son" Isaac to death, but receives him again "from the dead," crowned with a richer wealth of promise than ever he had heard before.[18] Joseph refuses to commit one great sin, and his refusal ends apparently in the loss of all hope of earthly happiness, and in the exchange of the high place of honor for a prison cell, but he becomes at last a prince in the land of Egypt.[19] Moses "chooses rather to be evil entreated with the people of God than to enjoy the pleasures of sin for a season; accounting the reproach of Christ greater riches than the treasures of Egypt," and he becomes the leader and lawgiver of a nation, and makes to himself an immortal name in the history of the world.[20] Daniel is true to God in the midst of the seductions of a heathen court, although his fidelity seemed to close every path of worldly advancement against him, but he rises to the chief place in the land, and is "ruler over the whole province of Babylon, and chief of the governors over all the wise men of Babylon."[21]

And thus the great law of the Master, that "whosoever would save his life shall lose it, and whosoever shall lose his life . . . shall save it," fulfills itself in human experience. Honesty is the best policy, but it is only so on condition it is pursued not as a policy, but as a principle. We gain what we lose, and more than we lose, in the path of duty, but only on condition that we are not thinking of the gain, but of the duty, when we make the sacrifice it entails. The rewards of righteousness

---

[18] Genesis 22:15, *seq.*
[19] Genesis 39
[20] Hebrews 11:24–26
[21] Daniel 2:48

disappear the moment they are made the conditions and motives of righteousness: they return in overflowing measure to those who, in their passion for righteousness, have forgotten altogether whether it has rewards or not. "There is no man that hath left house, or brethren, or sisters, or mother, or father, or children, or lands, for My sake, and for the Gospel's sake, but he shall receive a hundredfold NOW IN THIS TIME houses, and brethren, and sisters, and mothers, and children, and lands, with persecutions; and in the world to come eternal life."[22]

One last office remained to the angels in their ministry to their Lord. They had watched, may we not say, with deep and reverent awe the long conflict of forty days of Christ with Satan; they had beheld Him triumphant over every form of temptation; they had seen how His victory had been won at the cost to Himself of sore weakness and exhaustion; they had been permitted to come to this earth to minister to His need; and now, "home on joyful wings," they celebrate His triumphs on high.

Satan had assaulted "the Prince and Savior" of the world with his deadliest force, but had failed, and if we may faintly imagine the terror and dismay which his defeat must have caused in the realms of his own infernal kingdom, we may also imagine the exultant gladness with which the tidings of the victory of the great "Captain of our salvation" must have filled the courts of heaven, as they echoed with the shout of triumph, "Sing unto the Lord, for He hath triumphed gloriously:" "The Lord is a man of war; the Lord is His name; Thy right hand, O Lord, is glorious in power; Thy right hand hath dashed in pieces the enemy:" "The Lord shall reign for ever and ever."

But the warfare of Christ against sin is not yet completed. He has never laid down the glorious work which He began when "He was led up of the Spirit into the wilderness to be tempted of the devil." He will not lay it down till "the last enemy shall be abolished," and "all things are put in subjection under His feet."

Blessed, thrice blessed, they who in this holy war have taken sides

---

[22] Mark 10:29–30

with Christ, and have sworn, as with an oath, that they too will not rest until all sin, whether within themselves or in the sinful world without, shall be destroyed, and "God shall be all in all."

"There hath no temptation taken you but such as man can bear: but God is faithful, who will not suffer you to be tempted above that ye are able; but will with the temptation make also the way of escape, that ye may be able to endure it."
1 Corinthians 10:13

"Apart from me ye can do nothing."
John 15:5

"I can do all things in him that strengtheneth me."
Philippians 4:13

"I live, and yet no longer I, but Christ liveth in me."
Galations 2:20

"Be strong in the Lord, and in the strength of his might."
Ephesians 6:10

"He that overcometh, I will give to him to sit down with me in my throne, as I also overcame, and sat down with my Father in his throne."
Revelation 3:21

# X

## CHRIST'S VICTORY: THE PLEDGE AND POWER OF OUR VICTORY OVER TEMPTATION AND SIN

WE have already seen that temptation, even of the fiercest kind, need not imply a fallen state. The temptations of Christ are not only the proof that sin in no way necessarily follows previous temptation, but they are also the proof that temptation in no way necessarily implies previous sin. Temptation, in fact, is an inevitable condition and result of probation; and had man never fallen he would still have required the searching discipline of trial, for until goodness is proved it can never be assured of its own reality and stability.

In this light Christ's temptations may be regarded as types of the temptations through which each man would have passed if sin had never "entered into the world, and death through sin," and His victories as types of the victories man would have gained over sin. The whole of the life of our Lord indeed was a representative life, as truly as His death was a representative death for human sin. As "the Son of Man," His life was the realized ideal of the Divine Image in which man was originally created, but which had been lost through his fall. Even the great facts of the Incarnation and Resurrection, which stand at the commencement and the close of the human life of the Lord Jesus, have their relation to us as well as to Him. In the suggestive words of Canon Westcott,[1] "the Incarnation gives the absolute pledge of the fulfillment of man's destiny: the Resurrection shows that fulfillment

---
[1] Westcott, Brooke Foss (1881). *The Revelation of the Risen Lord*, Preface (p. xiii).

already attained, as far as our present powers enable us to realize the truth. So it is that Christ, as raised from the dead, is spoken of as 'the second Adam,' in whom men are reborn, and also as 'the head of the body, the Church.' The Resurrection, as answering to death, so far depended on the fall, but the glory of the Risen Lord, answering to the accomplishment of the Idea in which man was created, is independent of it. We see in the Risen Christ the end for which man was made, and the assurance that the end is within reach. The Resurrection, if we may so speak, shows us the change which would have passed over the earthly life of man if sin had not brought in death."

We may take these last words and apply them with equal truth to the victories which Christ gained over the temptations of the devil. If His temptations are the ideal forms under which sinless humanity, if it had remained loyal to God, would have had to meet temptation, His victories are types and illustrations of the successive conquests man would have won over temptation had he never fallen. The tree of forbidden fruit, as we have said, would have been found in every garden, but any garden would have been a paradise, and a paradise never "lost" through transgression.

But the race, alas! has fallen. We have sinned, and in our revolt against the authority and love of God, have brought disaster and death on ourselves, and the question at once arises, whether the victories of our Lord over the devil have therefore lost their significance to the life of fallen humanity? Is the rich and glorious promise they would have afforded to us, as a sinless race, of a life of victory over temptation unchecked and untarnished by a single defeat, emptied of all its meaning now that we have "sinned and fallen short of the glory of God"?

To this question the teaching of the New Testament, and the experience of innumerable generations of saints, return an unhesitating response. As the life of Jesus still remains, even to sinful man, at once the revelation and the example of the glory still possible to him in his fallen state, so the triumph of the Lord Jesus over the tempter is the pledge and prophecy of His final triumph over sin. "If we endure" — either suffering or temptation with Him — "we shall also reign with Him."

To say that the Christian has to struggle against temptation and sin is only to say half the truth. The Christian has not only to struggle, he has to overcome. Victory, not defeat, is to be the normal condition of the Christian life. The temptations to sin which beset us are as various as human character itself; they may come to the soul from the intellect or the affections quite as much as from "the world, the flesh, and the devil," but the issue of the conflict is to be the same in every case. We have an armor wherewith we are "able to stand against the wiles of the devil,"[24] and a shield wherewith we are "able to quench all the fiery darts of the evil one."[25] This is the ideal of the Christian conflict; why is it that in actual experience we come so far short of the ideal? There are children of God who ought long ago to have been freed from the bondage of evil habit or the tyranny of besetting sin, but instead of this, the power of the habit over them seems hardly broken, and the sin still fills them with sorrow and shame as they remember how often they have struggled against it in vain. Why is this melancholy experience so common? In the great majority of cases, because they have never yet learned the secret of the Christian life. They strive, and strive honestly, against temptation and sin, but they strive, looking to Christ rather to supplement the deficiencies of their own moral strength, than to fill them with His own Divine and victorious power in the conflict. They do what they can, and when they fail, they ask Christ to help them; but they never dream of doing nothing at all except to cast themselves from the first wholly on their Lord, and emptied of all confidence in their own power to resist sin, to appeal to Him to fight in them and for them, because "the battle is not theirs, but the Lord's." Or to put the same truth in another form. Christian people never doubt that the Lord Jesus Christ, through His Holy Spirit, stands in some relation to their will, but if they were to ask themselves what relation it is that Christ thus sustains to them, they would answer that it is an indirect and instrumental relation. They believe, that is, that Christ influences them through His word, or in the acts of Christian worship, or in the sacrament of the Lord's Supper, or by the discipline

---

[24] Ephesians 6:11
[25] Ephesians 6:16

of life, but they do not believe, or at least they do not realize the fact, that He also stands in a more immediate and direct relation to their souls than one human soul can stand to another: that He is able directly and personally to communicate of His own exhaustless might to the broken will, so that even the feeblest Christian may rejoice to say, "The strength of Christ may rest upon me."

The result is seen in those failures and defeats in the Christian life with which we are all, alas! too familiar, and which are sometimes so frequent as to reverse the true order of Christian experience, and to make victory the exception rather than the rule.

We have not yet fully learned "the unsearchable riches of Christ." He has already done more for us than in the beginnings of our Christian life we could have believed it possible even for Him to do, but He has not yet accomplished all His "good pleasure" in us. We have yet to learn what is the "exceeding greatness of His power to us-ward who believe."[26] We may come nearer to Him, and He may come nearer to us than we think. His own parable of "the Vine," and "the branches;" His own words, "Abide in Me, and I in you, for apart from Me ye can do nothing," may be translated into the daily but blessed reality of the Christian life. It is impossible to expect Him to do too much for us when He has Himself told us, "He that believeth on Me, the works that I do shall he do also; and greater works than these shall he do; because I go unto the Father."[27]

But this supreme triumph of the power of God in us, which is the one unfading ideal of the Christian life, never reached but ever before everyone who has "known the Lord," is impossible unless we are prepared to fulfill the conditions on which that power descends on the human soul.

And of these the first and simplest, and yet perhaps the most difficult, is the confession of our own helplessness and impotence. It is the emptied vessel which alone can be filled with the grace of God, and until we are emptied of all self-confidence, and realize in the depths of our own soul the meaning of the Master's words, "Apart from Me

---

[26] Ephesians 1:18–19
[27] John 14:12

ye can do nothing," it is vain for us to expect the fullness of His power to rest upon us. In a little village in Switzerland there stands a Roman Catholic Church, the whiteness of whose spire shines above the dark-roofed chalets around, and on the wall behind and above the altar within the church, there is painted a rude picture of the crucified Christ, of the kind so commonly seen in Catholic churches on the continent. Below the figure of Christ there is written the single word "I" in German, but some of the drops of blood which have fallen from the pierced hands and side have splashed on that "Ich," and have struck it through as with a crimson line. That village artist had learned "the secret of Jesus," that "he that loseth his life" for Christ's sake "shall find it;" and not until we have learned the same lesson, and discover, perhaps after many humbling defeats and much painful experience, that it is as impossible to trust self too little, as it is to trust Christ too much, shall we find the secret of a life of victory over sin in the words, "I live, yet no longer I, but Christ liveth in Me."

But this appeal to the strength of Christ can only be made "by faith," and faith in Christ is as essential a condition of the exercise of His power as distrust of self.

In the prayer of St. Paul for the Ephesian Church which has been already quoted, he asks God that they may know "the exceeding greatness of His power *to us-ward who believe*," as if even the answer to his prayer was limited by their faith. And it is so. It has been one of the saddest misfortunes to Christian truth that this one act of the soul which Christ and His apostles have made the condition, not only of personal salvation, but of the reception of those large and precious gifts which Christ has ascended to bestow on all who trust in Him, has been so often degraded, largely through the indiscretions and exaggerations of ignorant but well-meaning evangelists, into a mechanical and meaningless fetish. When faith in the Lord Jesus Christ has been made to mean little more than the utterance of the words, "I believe," "I do believe," as if there was magic even in the sound of the words, it is little wonder if the skeptical and critical have scornfully asked how a talisman like that can open the treasures of the kingdom of heaven to the soul.

Faith is no such fetish as this. It is the supreme act of the soul; the synthesis of all its powers; the union of thought, of feeling, of will, in one critical and glowing response to the offer of Christ; the submission of the whole man to His authority and love; the uplifted and emptied human hand which receives "the gift of God." "By faith," to use only a few of the great Scriptural words concerning it, we are "grafted in" to Christ;[28] "through faith" Christ "dwells in our hearts;"[29] "by faith" we have "access into this grace wherein we stand;"[30] "by faith" we are "begotten of God;"[31] nay! so limitless is its power that our Lord Himself declares "All things are possible to him that believeth."[32]

This is faith, and such faith we must have if we are ever to conquer temptation, and to be saved from our sins. It is not because Christ's power is exhausted that we so often fail in the conflicts of the Christian life; it is because we have not yet learned to trust Him as He deserves to be trusted. If "all things are possible to faith," it almost seems as if all things were possible to unbelief, for it can limit omnipotence itself, so that even of Christ it can be said, "He could do there no mighty work, and He marveled because of their unbelief."[33] To us His own question comes as it came to the blind men of old, before He can do for us any miracle of grace, "Believe ye that I am able to do this?" and to us, as to them, He still declares the great law of His power, "According to your faith be it done unto you."[34]

But even this is not all. This undivided trust in the power of Christ does not supersede that moral discipline of ourselves which is an essential condition of all true holiness of character and of life. Not only is faith in Christ not inconsistent with such a discipline, but the discipline itself is one of the conditions of a strong and triumphant faith. For, as has already been observed, faith is not a mechanical

---

[28] Romans 11:20, 23
[29] Ephesians 3:17
[30] Romans 5:2
[31] 1 John 5:1, 18
[32] Mark 9:23
[33] Mark 6:5, 6
[34] Matthew 9:28–29

act, it is the highest moral attitude of the soul to God; and if so, this attitude must be determined in the last resort by the moral condition of the soul itself. To imagine that because nothing but faith in Christ is required to enable us to overcome sin, we may be careless of ourselves, may venture perilously near danger, may "enter into temptation," may abandon watching and self-denial and prayer, may forgo all that inward disciplining of self which St. Paul says is part of the "gift of God,"[35] is to imagine we may sow the seeds of the flesh and reap the fruits of the spirit. The one perfect example which the world has ever seen of faith, the Lord Jesus Himself, has not only revealed to us the triumphs possible to faith, but He has also shown us the secret places where alone these triumphs are won. He lived a life of constant watching and self-discipline and prayer; He "pleased not Himself;"[36] His cross was so constantly with Him that He said, "If any man would come after Me, let him deny himself daily and follow Me;"[37] and He found in prolonged communion with God, the nourishment and strengthening of His own spiritual life. He entered on His public ministry with prayer;[38] He repaired the exhaustion of spiritual work by "rising up a great while before day" to pray;[39] He "continued all night in prayer to God," before choosing the twelve apostles and founding His Church among men;[40] He met temptation twice over with watching and prayer;[41] He enters both the way of the Cross and the glory of the Transfiguration through prayer;[42] He begins His passion with prayer;[43] He dies with the words of prayer on His

---

[35] 2 Timothy 1:7, Σωφρονισμός.
[36] Romans 15:3
[37] Luke 9:23
[38] Luke 3:21
[39] Mark 1:35, compare with Luke 5:16 , and the next verse.
[40] Luke 6:12–13
[41] Matthew 14:23 compared with John 6:15; and for the second time, Matthew 26:36, 40.
[42] Luke 9:18, and Luke 9:28.
[43] Luke 22:40–41

lips.[44] This is the life of "the Leader and Perfecter of the Faith,"[45] a life from which we learn that the most watchful self-discipline, the most constant self-denial, the most fervent prayer, are only the human conditions of that fullness of Faith, which in its turn becomes the condition of the fullness of the Power of God.

But with these conditions fulfilled on our part, it is hard to say how much God may not do for us. The doctrine of "perfectionism," whether in the more ancient form set up by Pelagianism,[46] or in the more modern form it took in the teaching of Wesley,[47] and which has been reproduced without the qualifications Wesley gave to it, and the balance his ethical teaching afforded, in a crude and perilous form by the "Salvation Army," has always been discredited in the Church, not less by its general common sense, than by the teaching of Scripture, and by a profounder philosophy of sin. But erroneous, and oftentimes dangerous, as this doctrine is, it is not wholly error. It would never have lived in the Church of Christ, it would never have exerted so potent a spell as it has over the coarse and uneducated natures who have been taught by the Salvation Army that they may pass at one bound, from a life of bestiality and wickedness into the possession of a "clean heart," had it not contained, however mixed with error, a great truth — the truth that when the moral conditions of the reception of the grace of God are perfectly fulfilled, there is no triumph over temptation and sin impossible to man, because there is none impossible to God.

The Church of Christ has too much been allowed to regard defeats in the warfare against sin as part of the normal condition of the

---

[44] Luke 23:46

[45] Hebrews 12:2. It is with great diffidence that I venture to differ from the Revised Version, but surely the revisers, by the insertion of the word "our" in italics in this verse, have misconceived its true meaning. The writer is not speaking of Jesus as the "author of *our* faith," but as the one perfect Example of faith to whom we are to "look" while we "run with patience the race set before us." The words which follow are enough to show that he is thinking of Christ's life as the life of the "Leader and Perfecter of Faith."

[46] The theological doctrine of Pelagius (c. 360–418 AD) and his followers, in particular the denial of the doctrines of original sin and predestination, and the defense of innate human goodness and free will.

[47] John Wesley (1703–1791), an English cleric and theologian who co-founded Methodism.

Christian life, instead of as a shame, and a disaster, and a sin. When victory over temptation has come, it has too often come as a surprise to the soul; and gloomy acquiescence in lifelong weakness or sin has taken the place of the shout of triumph, "Thanks be to God who giveth us the victory through our Lord Jesus Christ."

It is unnecessary to say we shall never wholly conquer sin, or be "made perfect" in this present life. The conditions necessary for the soul to be so filled with God as to make sin impossible will never be perfectly realized on earth. It is not a little thing, nevertheless, to know what God can do for us, if we will only wholly trust Him; it is not a little thing to have ever shining before us the promise which Christ has made our own, which is being fulfilled in this life in spite of its sorrows, and failures, and defeats, and which will crown us with immortal blessedness in the triumphs of the eternal world — the promise that He will "bruise Satan under our feet,"[48] and "will guard us from stumbling, and set us before the presence of His glory without blemish in exceeding joy."[49]

The glory of that final triumph over sin will be His, not ours; but even here on earth we may in part anticipate its glory, and join in the song of those whom He has made "more than conquerors," "UNTO HIM THAT IS ABLE TO DO EXCEEDING ABUNDANTLY ABOVE ALL THAT WE ASK OR THINK, ACCORDING TO THE POWER THAT WORKETH IN US, UNTO HIM BE THE GLORY IN THE CHURCH AND IN CHRIST JESUS UNTO ALL GENERATIONS FOR EVER AND EVER. AMEN."[50]

---

[48] Romans 16:20
[49] Jude 24
[50] Ephesians 3:20–21

**REV. GEORGE SLATYER BARRETT, D.D.**
HONORARY HEATHEN

**NO MAN IS A SERVANT OF GOD WHO HAS NOT LEARNED THAT THE ESSENCE OF ALL GOODNESS LIES IN PUTTING GOD BEFORE SELF.**

www.ingramcontent.com/pod-product-compliance
Lightning Source LLC
Chambersburg PA
CBHW021440080526
44588CB00009B/616